You're Strong Enough

A Quest to Discover Who You Really Are

By

Kassi L. Pontious

ENLIGHTEN ME PUBLISHING
Highland, Utah

Book Design by Expert Subjects, LLC
Interior Design by Steven James Catizone
Editing by Gail Lennon

Library of Congress Control Number: 2013941978

You're Strong Enough Color Version
ISBN-10: 098954270X
ISBN-13: 978-0-9895427-0-8

You're Strong Enough B/W Version
ISBN-10: 0989542718
ISBN-13: 978-0-9895427-1-5

Printed in the United States of America

First Edition: July 2013
10 9 8 7 6 5 4 3 2 1

Contents

Acknowledgements

I want to thank my husband Dave for all his support and encouragement on this endeavor.

I want to thank my Heavenly Father for the inspiration and insights in developing this work to assist the youth in finding the truths of why they are here on Earth.

I also want to thank those that assisted me in completing this work, namely my editors, designer Steven James Catizone and family and friends.

Preface
The Day I Felt Strong Enough

We are all on a quest here on Earth to find out who we are and what we're made of. As a result, we will encounter many hardships during our life. Some hardships will seem like small hills, while others will appear to be huge mountains. I'd like to share with you one of the most difficult mountains I had to climb to remove myself from an unhealthy and dangerous situation.

As the eleventh of twelve children, I never felt part of a family. My parents got a divorce when I was four years old. My father stayed in California and my mother took the youngest eight of us to Utah, where her parents lived. My mom felt so out of control because of the divorce that there was constant fighting over cleanliness, our personal direction and getting back at my dad by using us as pawns.

After the divorce my mom pushed each of her children into sports to help them stay out of trouble. I personally started playing tennis in Provo, Utah at age ten. I became very good extremely fast so my mom moved me down to California to train with the best coaches.

In California, I lived with three different families (not knowing any of them) and went to two different schools. After a year of training, my mom moved out to be with me. Tennis went from being enjoyable to being a living hell because my mom demanded perfection from me. I got screamed at constantly and sometimes hit if I lost a match. As a result of my mother's pressure and her abuse towards me, I felt that I had no other option except to leave this world. Fortunately, through divine intervention, my mind was changed. A couple of months later, I still felt I had to do something to save myself from this hell. So, at age fourteen, I ran away from home.

After the year my mom moved out to California to watch me train to be a professional tennis player, we soon moved back home to Utah. I decided that I was sick of playing tennis because of all the pain I had to deal with from my mother's abuse. During those three months of summer, my mom did everything she could to get me to play tennis again, including, visiting with a leader from my church.

This leader was a world-class athlete. Therefore, my mother thought he could help change my mind and I would continue to play tennis. Her plan backfired. He asked what I wanted to do with my life and I told him I wanted to live with my dad. As soon as I told my mom I wanted to live with my dad, the fighting started up again.

One morning while I was eating breakfast, my mother started going at me again. She rehashed all that she had done for me and how ungrateful I was being. She yelled at me for about an hour. I just sat there and took it because I was soft-spoken, peaceful, non-contentious and non-argumentative.

After an hour of listening to her telling me what an ungrateful child I was for not playing tennis anymore, I tried to leave but my mother blocked the way. Finally, I said, "Excuse me. I'm trying to leave."

My mother responded, "There's no way you're leaving! I'm not done talking to you."

I said, "Well I need to leave because all you're doing is screaming at me and I need a break."

She replied, "There is no way you are leaving."

So I barely pushed her hip so I could get by her. That's when my mother grabbed my hair and threw me on the ground. After trying for ten minutes of struggling to get her off of me and stop pulling my hair, I finally pushed her off.

For a moment it was quiet, until my mother stood up and started screaming at me again. As I watched her yell at me, I saw in her eyes that nothing would ever change. I knew in that moment that she was out-of-control and it was only going to get worse. I felt in my gut that if I stayed, something bad would happen. So, I took off and started walking down our street.

A million thoughts went through my mind about what had just happened. Realizing the emotional trauma I just went through caused my hands to shake. Then I noticed in the corner of my eye my mom's car pull up beside me. She rolled down the window and said, "Why don't you get in the car and we will go get something to eat and talk?" My mom knew that I loved going out to eat and she knew that would be a huge temptation for me. For a moment I considered it, but then something inside of me more powerful than I'd ever felt before, said with a loud voice, "RUN!"

I ran as fast as I could. As I was running, a voice inside of me said again, "Go over to that church building." Once I arrived at the church building, I started checking all the doors to see if any of them were unlocked. No luck. My heart was pounding and I was so scared. I was afraid my mother would catch me before I could get inside. As I was checking all the doors again, my mom drove around the corner of the building and looked right at me. Then, slowly, she continued to drive forward as if she had not seen me at all. As I stood there in awe, someone came out of the church door and I was able to squeeze inside.

Once inside, I found a bunch of kids playing basketball in the gym and then I noticed a phone on the wall and the thought came to me to call my sister. When I called, she answered and sounded surprised that I was calling her at work. She had been fired three days previously and was just there picking up her stuff. As I was telling my sister what was happening, I heard banging on the door. I saw my mom checking all the doors trying to get in. To my relief, no one heard her, so she left. My sister instructed me to meet her at her office four miles away. While I was hiding out at her office, both my brother and a police officer came to inquire about my whereabouts. My sister told both of them she didn't know where I was, though I was hiding in the back bathroom, so each of them left.

We left for my sister's home soon after. While my sister was getting ready for the evening, another person came to the front door, but I did not answer. A couple of minutes later a knock came to the back sliding door; I still did not answer, so the door started sliding open. To my relief, it stopped because of a stick in the tracking system. After this third attempt of someone trying to find me, I broke down and cried.

At dinner that night, I expressed my feelings of fear and the disappointment that mom had in me. I related to my sister all that had transpired, including the miracles that kept me safe. I told her about the voice inside that told me to run and go to the building; the miracle that my mom could not see me when she drove right past me; the door opening for me and not for her; that my sister was at her office when she had been fired; the prompting to memorize your number three days previously; that the cop did not search the building for me because I was a runaway and how the sliding glass door stopped from opening when someone came looking for me here.

My sister listened carefully and commented: "Kassi, do you realize how many miracles happened to you so that you could run away from mom? Can you see that that's an answer from God? It is time to leave mom. It will be safer for you to be with dad." After she put it into perspective, I felt at peace and agreed with her.

My sister contacted my dad and made arrangements for me to fly to California. I was thrilled and scared at the same time. I knew my mom would have photos of me at the airport. My sister sensed how frightened I was of going to jail if I was caught, so she devised a plan.

She came up with a disguise for me that made me look much older and completely different. My disguise included: full makeup, high heels, stuffed bra and tight dress. As we were arriving at the airport, my sister told me she put the name on the ticket as "Morgan Bond" like James Bond.

When I got to the security check, I noticed that the security officers were looking at me weird. I was so relieved when they let me pass through. Once in the air I felt this complete peace and excitement fill my soul. I was free at last from the abuse I had suffered for three years. It was the beginning of living my life, not my mother's. I knew from that experience that I was strong enough, that God would perform miracles as we need them, and that we are never alone here on Earth.

I share this experience to give the reader an idea of the struggles we each have, though different in nature, and that we are strong enough to get through. This book is not about dishonoring your parents. I honored my mother enough to ask her permission in sharing my stories in this book and she said, "Yes." She and I both know it was a bad time for both of us. No parent intentionally tries to destroy their children's lives. They are human and are just trying to survive themselves in this dysfunctional world. This book is about knowing why you are here and believing you are strong enough for whatever happens to you in your life.

We are each placed on this Earth to conquer and overcome all obstacles that are placed in our path. Each of us is strong enough for anything we go through. With God's help, anything is possible—including being happy here on Earth despite our trials and challenges.

If I am Strong Enough, So Are You!

Introduction

Chere is a purpose and plan for everyone and you are strong enough for yours. In this book, *You're Strong Enough,* you will discover who you really are and that this Earthly life is a test. A test to prove ourselves to our Heavenly Father that we are strong enough for anything that is placed along our path and worthy enough to receive our reward.

You're Strong Enough will take you on a quest to discover where you came from, why you are here, and what your ultimate goal is. You will learn how to conquer the dragon that is trying to destroy your life by using the gifts and talents you were given. You will find out how to cut the strings of dysfunction that are trying to control your life.

You're Strong Enough will teach you what tools are available to you to overcome any trial or challenge you are faced with. *You're Strong Enough* will also bring perspective on who made the world dysfunctional, why we have self-esteem problems, how anger clouds our views and what bad habits thwart our divine destiny.

At the end of each chapter, you will go on a quest to discover who you really are and why you are here. Each new discovery will bring you closer to the life you were born to live and the peace you may be searching for. You will come to find you are strong enough to defeat the dragon and conquer your ultimate quest.

Let the Quest Begin!

The Quest Begins

CHAPTER I

The Quest Begins
Discover where you came from

O nce upon a time, in a far-off land where freedom reigned, love abounded, and joy filled the air, there lived a king and a queen.

This king and queen had many children—thousands in fact. Each one had a divine nature, and an individual worth. The king and queen loved each of their children very much.

All of the children grew to full stature and complete understanding that they were of royal birth. Each son and daughter knew they had the potential to become a king or a queen themselves. But, the children were limited in discovering their true potential while living at home with their mom and dad, the king and queen of the land.

Each of them had to go on a quest. A quest for knowledge, a quest for understanding, a quest for growth, a quest to discover, through trials and challenges, to discover their true identity and what kingdom they might obtain.

This quest began with a choice: to be forced to follow the king's plan unquestioningly or to opt for free agency to choose if they would follow the king's plan or not.

Pre-Earthly Life

The far-off place was called the Preexistence. The king and queen I am referring to are our Heavenly Father, or God, and our Heavenly Mother. The children born to this king and queen are all of us here on Earth. Each of us is, literally, a son or daughter of God. We have the potential of being and having everything our parents have as king and queen.

Since each of us is a son or daughter of God, we each are of royal birth. So we have the potential of, one day, being a king or queen over our own land. In Romans 8:17 the Bible tells us, "And if children, then heirs; heirs of God, and joint-heirs with Christ." Also in Ps. 82:6 it states, "I have said, 'Ye are gods; and all of you are children of the most high.'"

Before we came to this Earthly life, each of us lived with our Heavenly Father and Mother in a place called Preexistence. Here, each of us had a spirit body. We were, literally, the spirit children of Heavenly parents, each an individual with a divine nature and destiny. In Numbers 16:22, the Bible tells us that "...God is the God of the spirits of all flesh" and thus our First Father.

Each of us grew, learned and loved being with our Heavenly Father, but our joy was limited. To become like our Heavenly Father, we must have a physical body like He does and be tested to see if we are worthy of having everything He had. Our Heavenly Father tells us in Matt 5:48, "Be ye therefore perfect, even as your Father which is in Heaven is perfect..." In this scripture He is telling us to succeed as He has succeeded. Such success starts with conquering our Earthly quest.

Therefore, our Heavenly Father devised a plan, or a quest, that each of us must go on in order to prove to our Heavenly Father that through knowledge, experience, integrity, character, and love we were worthy of obtaining our own throne. This quest or plan is called the plan of salvation. In Moses 1:39, God declares to us this plan through His mission statement, "For behold, this is my work and my glory—to bring to pass the immortality and eternal life of man." As stated, this plan of God's has two purposes. One is to receive a physical body (immortality) and then be resurrected and the second is to use free agency to obtain eternal life.

This quest would take place outside the castle, high up in the clouds, in a place called Earth. Earth is where we would receive a physical body and be tested to see if we would freely choose good over evil. When we first found out about this plan, or the quest, we would go on to achieve everything our Father in Heaven had achieved as king; we were so thrilled to go. As stated in Job 38:7, "…and all the sons of God shouted for joy."

Each of us knew we could only learn so much in our spirit bodies. The real test came with free agency and physical bodies. Though we were excited to go on this new quest full of adventure and learning, we also knew with this quest came with a risk. A risk that darkness would cloud our view of our divine destiny and, as a result of such darkness, make us unable to live with our Father in Heaven again.

Because of the dangers of the quest, we knew someone needed to go before us to show us how to complete this quest, how to overcome evil and provide a way for us to come back home to our Heavenly Father if the darkness made us lose our way.

Upon discussing the quest that each of us would need to go on in order to obtain a throne as a prince or princess, our Heavenly Father welcomed ideas from His older sons, Jesus Christ and Lucifer, for this task.

Lucifer spoke first. He said, "Send me. I know they have to receive a physical body in order to achieve what you have, Father. But, don't give them their free agency. They will just screw it up. I will force them to do what is right on their individual quests. When I force them to do what is right and to execute the quest perfectly, you will not lose one child. I will do all of this on one condition: I want all your power and glory." You can find this statement in Moses 4:1, "Behold, here am I, send me,

I will be thy son, and I will redeem all mankind, that one soul shall not be lost, and surely I will do it; wherefore give me thine honor."

After Lucifer spoke, Jesus Christ came forth. He said, "Send me, Father. Once your children receive their physical bodies, they will need someone to guide and direct them through the obstacle course on their individual quests. Give them their free agency, for there is power in personal choice. Though they may make mistakes and fall off the path during their quests, I will die for them and be the sacrifice for their sins and mistakes so that when they do fall off they can still return to you and be a prince or princess of the land. I will go down to Earth and live among them. I will learn as they will learn and I will suffer and feel all the pains they will feel. I will go first and do the obstacle course that they, too, must later go through. I will be spit on, jabbed at and even nailed to the Cross for them."

Jesus added, "I will go through every imaginable experience that all my brothers and sisters could possibly go through, because I love them and they are my family."

The Bible tells us of His sacrifice in Isa. 53:5, "But he was wounded for our transgressions, he was bruised for our iniquities: the chastisement of our peace was upon him; and with his stripes we are healed."

Jesus continues, "I will go through the pains and suffering for them, not only so that they can return to their Father and be victorious in their quest, but so they may know that I understand what they're going through in their past and in their present."

"Father, as they repent and pick themselves up when they have fallen down or become lost in the darkness through mistakes and sins, they will be forgiven. I will also heal and bring peace and comfort to the souls of those who have gotten hurt innocently. And, Father, all the glory will be Yours."

This is referenced in Moses 4:2, "But, behold, my Beloved Son, which was my Beloved and Chosen from the beginning, said unto me—Father, thy will be done, and the glory be thine forever."

After our Heavenly Father, the king, had listened to both of His sons and their proposed solutions, He chose the second son, Jesus Christ, who offered to go down to Earth on His own quest to suffer for the sins and mistakes of the world (because of free agency) and to die so that all might be resurrected and live again.

Our Heavenly Father chose Jesus Christ's offer because He knew each one of His children had to overcome trials and challenges on their own. That was the best way to learn how to be a prince or a princess worthy of a throne. God knew He would never be able to tell who loved Him or wanted to be a true heir to the throne if they were forced to do what is right. He knew if you were forced to do what is right, you would never build character, learn and grow, and be victorious on your own quest and thus proving yourself to be a good king or queen.

Upon hearing the King's decision, Lucifer became furious. He convinced one-third of our Heavenly Father's children to rebel against our Heavenly Father's choice. This rebellion and contention caused a war in Heaven (not a war with blood, but a war over free agency). This war is referenced in Rev. 12:7, "And there was war in heaven: Michael and his angels fought against the dragon [*Lucifer*]; and the dragon fought and his angels,"

This war involved all of our Heavenly Father's children. Each child had to make a choice for free agency and God's plan, or to be forced to do what is right, Satan's plan. All those who chose free agency and God's plan were known as warriors of light. As a result, upon victory, they would be knighted with a body for their valiancy and given the opportunity to take part in an individual quest.

When the Lord was victorious, Lucifer and his followers were cast out and Lucifer then became Satan. Satan is the father of all lies, the author of deception, and the dragon of darkness. He is our enemy, the one we must defeat and conquer, so as to become victorious in our quest. The Bible states this in Rev 12:9, "And the great dragon was cast out, that old serpent, called the Devil, and Satan, which deceiveth the whole world: he was cast out into the earth, and his angels were cast out with him."

All those warriors of light (all of us) who chose Jesus Christ's offer and our Heavenly Father's plan were sent to Earth to begin their quest with a physical body, so that they might be tested and proven worthy as heirs in the Kingdom of God.

All those who followed Satan's plan also came to Earth. But they did not receive a physical body. Instead, they will remain eternally as spirits. Because these spirits will never receive a body, they are angry and miserable. They will do anything they can to make those of us who pass our first test (or first estate) as miserable as they are. In Jude 1:6, "And the angels which kept not their first estate, but left their own habitation, he hath reserved in everlasting chains under darkness unto the judgment of the great day." It states that those who followed Satan and didn't pass their first estate are to be in darkness for eternity.

This quest will not be easy, not only because we've never done it before or the obstacles may be hard, but because we must defeat the dragon, Satan. He will do everything he can to thwart our efforts, push us into dark forests, and fill our minds with anger, hate and revenge. He wants us to lose our chance of living with our Heavenly King, our Father and the God of the Earth. As stated in Moses 4:4, be careful for Satan will be fierce when trying to knock us down, "And he became Satan, yea, even the devil, the father of all lies, to deceive and to blind men, and to lead them captive at his will, even as many as would not hearken unto my voice."

Family

After our Heavenly Father chose Jesus Christ to be the Savior of the world and leader on the path that we must walk. He pulled each of us aside and gave us what was necessary to accomplish our individual quests. He knew that, after winning the war in Heaven and losing one-third of His children to Lucifer's deceptions, that Lucifer would not just let us use our free agency to choose good over evil. He would use it against us through temptation.

Therefore, our Heavenly Father made sure He made each of us strong enough to overcome anything we would ever face in our Earthly life, through our own mistakes or by Satan's evil designs. Our Heavenly Father told us He would provide everything we needed in order to return to Him and become the prince and princess He wants us to be. His first suggestion was for us to pick from our friends those we would want to be in our Earthly family. These Heavenly friends would be our greatest strength on Earth. He knew these Heavenly friends would have more influence on us and our life than any other humans could. They would bring out the best in us, and test us. God further explained, if they are true to their course, they would be our best companions on our personal Earthly quest.

> Our Heavenly Father helped us create our Earthly family
> because He knew we could not achieve our quest alone.

After He advised us and warned us about choosing our family, He cautioned that some family members would lose their way. They would make poor choices that might hurt us. We would need to do whatever we could to strengthen ourselves and other members of the family to keep them and ourselves safe. He reminded us that we would each bring unique talents and gifts to the table to encourage, uplift and strengthen the other members of our family. He also explained there would be times when it will be hard to love our family. He told us not to give up on each other; for Satan will do everything he can to destroy the family unit.

God then tells us that, once we choose our family, then our parents and siblings will always be our parents and siblings. Our Heavenly Father reminded us that we chose each other to assist each other on

Earth. Therefore, He told us to forgive them and love them with all our hearts for they, too, would be on a quest constantly fighting Satan, the dragon, while trying to stay true to their course. They too would be striving to receive all that Heavenly Father had promised them as a prince or princess in His Kingdom. As our Heavenly Father finished helping us create our family unit, He then expressed with a full tender heart to please help each other down on Earth for Satan is our enemy, NOT each other.

Parents

As we were creating this family, our Heavenly Father asked us to take special care in choosing our parents. Our parents would be sent first to Earth, to learn how to fight the dragon. They would be able to experience life first, with all the ups and downs in relationships, finances, health, sickness, joy, pain and love. They can teach us and give us guidance and advice on what would help or hinder our life while completing our quest. Ultimately, our parents would teach us what would make us happy and what would make us miserable.

Father encourages us during our quest to counsel with our parents, talk with them, listen to them and to trust them. As parents, their main job is to teach and to instruct us about good and evil.

God also wants us to remember that there are always consequences of poor choices and rewards for good choices. Our job, as kids, is to learn and grow while watching our parents as role models. He further tells us that some of our parents would lose their way. If that happens, we are to look to other good adult role models as examples.

Our Heavenly Father reminds us that when our parents are doing the best they can they will be our greatest assets on Earth. He asks us to remember, when we get angry at them that we chose them as parents.

He urges us to be patient with them and forgive them when they make choices that are wrong or hurtful.

After discussing family and parents, our Heavenly Father gave us some gifts and talents to increase our chances of being successful on our quest. Each quest is individually suited for our ultimate growth. At times, we will be tested to the brink of our capacity. So, our Heavenly Father gave us everything we would need to conquer and overcome the dragon, Satan. He gave us talents to enjoy and enhance our journey, and gifts to overcome the obstacles. After bestowing upon us the gifts and talents we would need for the scratches and cuts we may encounter on our quest, our Heavenly Father then placed a set of armor in front of us that, if used, will ensure our success.

The Armor of God

ARMOUR OF GOD

EPHESIANS 6:11

"PUT ON THE WHOLE ARMOUR OF GOD, THAT YE MAY BE ABLE TO STAND AGAINST THE WILES OF THE DEVIL."

The armor of God is the added protection we will need to defeat and endure the fiery dragon (Satan) that awaits us on Earth. This armor is spoken of in Eph. 6:11, "Put on the whole Armour of God, that ye may be able to stand against the wiles of the devil."

Our Heavenly Father presents us with the sword of the spirit, the helmet of salvation, the shield of faith, the breastplate of righteousness, the belt of truth and the shoes of the Gospel. He explains that each piece combined will assist us on our quest through the obstacle course of our life.

Before explaining each piece, our Heavenly Father warns us that we will encounter temptation, anger, hurt, betrayal, divorce, depression and many other feelings of darkness that can thwart our success and happiness. Therefore, our Heavenly Father counsels us to use all the armor of God constantly throughout our lives because Satan wants us to be miserable and lose our eternal reward.

The Sword of the Spirit

Heb. 4:12, "For the word of God is quick, and powerful, and sharper than any two edged sword..."

The sword of the spirit is the Word of God, as mentioned in Heb. 4:12, "For the word of God is quick, and powerful, and sharper than any two edged sword..."

Just as a sword is a weapon used to strike or defend against an enemy, the Word of God has power to destroy the dragon that lies waiting to destroy us with its fiery darts of lies. Our Heavenly Father has sent others before us (prophets and Jesus Christ the Savior) to write the Word of God (the Scriptures). As we follow the Scriptures—which tell us what to do, how to avoid obstacles, what road leads us back to God, and what cliffs and dark forests to avoid (i.e. sin and temptation)—we will be led safely home.

Our Heavenly Father tells us if we want to be successful on this quest, then we must read the manual (scripture) from the one (Jesus Christ The Savior) who conquered His quest before us. The Scriptures tell us everything we must do to defeat the dragon and conquer our quest successfully.

The Breastplate of Righteousness

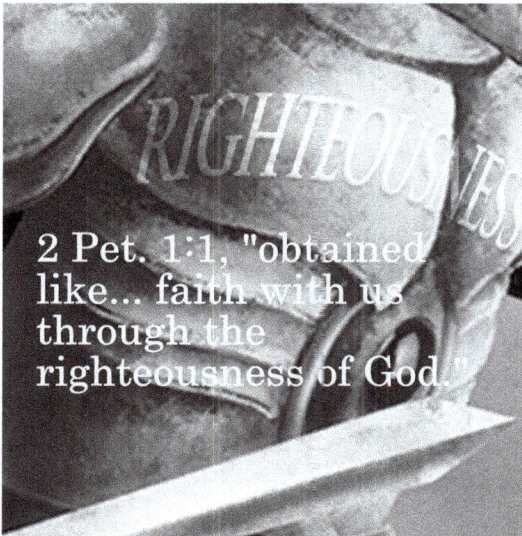

2 Pet. 1:1, "obtained like... faith with us through the righteousness of God."

A breastplate protects the most vital parts of our body, such as the heart and lungs. Similarly, righteous thoughts and deeds will protect us from the evil temptations of Satan. In 1 Cor. 15:34 it states, "Awake to righteousness, and sin not..." We must use the righteous example that comes from Jesus Christ and "sin not" to shield us from Satan.

Our Heavenly Father encourages us to keep our thoughts and minds clean from sin, lack of forgiveness, hate and revenge, so that we will be able to see the dangers on our path before they befall us. He warns us that, when we do not make righteous choices, we will be letting Satan be the puppeteer in our lives. Similarly, as we act and make good and righteous decisions, we will become stronger and, as we become stronger, we will be able to scare off the dragon for fear we will conquer Him again.

The Belt of Truth

TRUTH

Eph. 6:14, "Stand therefore, having your loins girt about with truth..."

The belt of truth defends us from Satan, the Father of Lies. If we are honest, as stated in John 8:32, "And ye shall know the truth, and the truth shall make you free," we will be made free. Free to follow the course our Heavenly Father sees for us, not the one Satan wants us to follow.

Just as belts are used in battle to strengthen the uniform as a whole and protect some very vital parts of our bodies, truth will keep us strong and true to whom we really are and what we can accomplish. Learning and holding onto the truths taught in the Scriptures (that we are of royal birth sent on a quest to prove ourselves) will help protect us from Satan's lies that we are worthless and not strong enough to endure. Holding onto truth and integrity will always set us free and keep us true to our course in our own life. Being true to yourself will allow you to keep your eyes on the road and never have to look back to see if the lie you told is following you. Truth will keep you from being distracted and falling off your path.

The Shoes of the Gospel

Eph. 6:15, "And your feet shod with the preparation of the gospel of peace;"

When going on a quest or battle against Satan, would you ever consider going without shoes? No, of course not! Shoes protect our feet against the different climates and surfaces we must climb on during our quest. Similarly, the Gospel of Jesus Christ (faith, hope, repentance, baptism…) is what will protect us against the evils designs and fiery lies of the dragon, Satan.

In Isa 52:7, it is written, "How beautiful upon the mountains are the feet of him that bringeth good tidings…" The good tidings are the Gospel the Savior brought to Earth while on His quest and is available to us today. His Gospel will keep us strong and unwavering when Satan and his angels try to attack us.

Shoes, like the gospel, will protect us in any circumstance or environment we encounter. If you want to finish this quest with honor and become a true prince or princess, you must be prepared to walk great heights to be like our Father in Heaven. Anyone can achieve great heights (live with God again) while defeating the dragon by embracing faith, repentance, baptism and the fullness of Christ's Gospel.

The Shield of Faith

Shields can be moved in many directions, blocking the evil forces and the weapons of our enemies. Similarly, faith is the ultimate shield on Earth. The importance of a shield is stated in Eph 6:16, "Above all, taking the shield of faith, wherewith ye shall be able to quench all the fiery darts of the wicked." This tells us that, with a shield of faith, we will not only dodge the fiery darts, but quench them. Faith is our

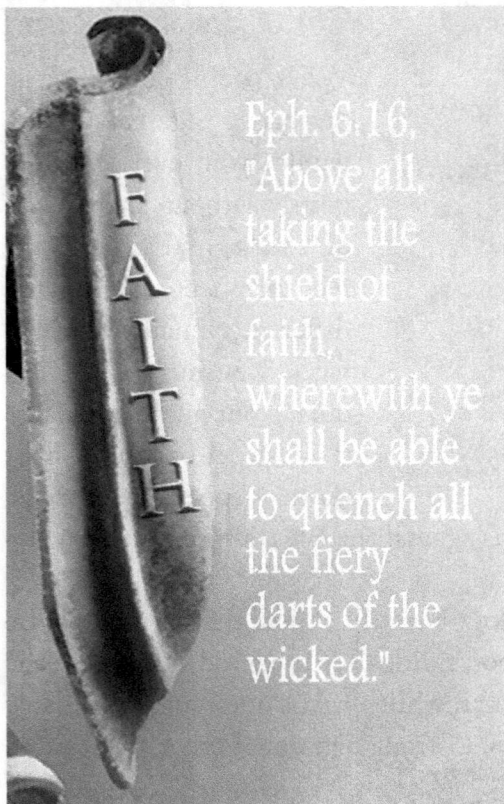

Eph. 6:16, "Above all, taking the shield of faith, wherewith ye shall be able to quench all the fiery darts of the wicked."

ultimate weapon against the dragon, for it will shield us against his deceptions and the fire of temptations.

As we have faith in Jesus Christ, who went before us, and our Heavenly Father's plan, we can know that all our efforts and energy on our quest will produce the ultimate victory of becoming a prince or princess at the right hand of God. Faith is believing that we are of royal birth and that God gave us what we would need to come back home victorious.

Faith has the power to move mountains, change hearts, heal souls and pave the pathway to return home. Faith is the shield that quenches the fiery darts of Satan. It is indispensable on our homeward quest.

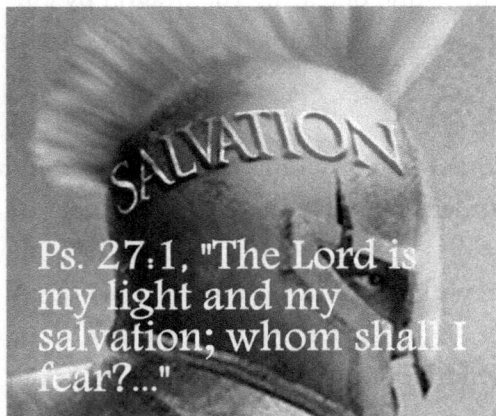

Ps. 27:1, "The Lord is my light and my salvation; whom shall I fear?..."

The Helmet of Salvation

Just as a helmet can protect the head from fatal wounds and severe brain damage, similarly, hope of salvation protects us from doubt, fear, and hopelessness. In Titus 1:2, "In hope of eternal life, which God, that cannot lie, promised before the world began," states we can be assured eternal life if we follow God's counsel and plan.

If we are sent on this quest to prove ourselves worthy of living in the Kingdom of God as a prince or princess and then are told by Satan that the quest isn't real, would you continue your quest? No. You would give up if you did not have hope for salvation. You must have hope that this quest is real and will lead to your just reward as prince or princess. That is why hope is compared to a helmet. Helmets are essential in any battle, as is hope essential during our quest for eternal life as heirs in God's Kingdom.

When our Heavenly Father presented us with the royal armor of God, He knew not all would receive it or use it when on Earth. He knew that many would think they could go on this quest with no protection at all. But, because He loved us so much, and since every human on Earth passed their first test as warriors of truth and freedom by being on the winning side of the war in Heaven, He wanted to give us some eternal gifts that would assist us on our individual quests. The first gift is called the light of Christ.

The Light of Christ

Our Heavenly Father explained that everyone on Earth will be given the light of Christ to guide them and help them discern good from evil in their life. This light would warn us of the poor choices we might encounter and any evil or danger that is on our path. It will be there as our conscience to guide us through our life and quest. He knew we were taking a risk leaving His presence, and not all would use the armor of God. Therefore, He wanted to make sure *everyone* was given an equal chance to find the truth about themselves, their quest (purpose) and His plan.

Our Heavenly Father explains that, though each of us will have this gift on Earth, it is still up to us to use the power of our free agency to make good choices. With the light of Christ, we can know whether the choices we are making are good or not. This light can illuminate the path we are taking in times of darkness.

Our Heavenly Father explains that the light of Christ is His way of helping us on this quest. The better the choices you make, the stronger the light (feelings) will get.

God then warns us that Satan will try to take away every gift God gives us. Therefore, the more we ignore those warning feelings, the quieter and dimmer the light of Christ becomes. If we continue to make wrong choices and ignore the light of Christ, soon it will disappear and we will find that we are walking aimlessly in the dark. On that day, the devil becomes our guide.

God counsels that the choice to listen to warning feelings is ours. He tells us that there is power in our choices. If we choose to listen to our conscience, then we are allowing our conscience to be more powerful, a brighter light on the pathway. If we ignore those warnings and discount the light of Christ, we are giving our power (agency) to Satan.

After explaining the benefits of the light of Christ and warning us of Satan, our Heavenly Father then asks who we will want to be our guide. Jesus Christ, who has our best interests at heart and will lead us to the Kingdom of God (happiness and safety), or, Satan who will take over our conscience and lead us to pain, suffering, unhappiness…and a failed, forgotten or lost quest?

Fruits of the Spirit

The second gift our Heavenly Father gave all His children on Earth is to know when truth is being spoken or read, and to know when we receive answers to our prayers. This gift is called the Spirit of God. When you feel the Spirit of God, you are feeling truth, a confirmation that you are doing what is right, that the answer to the question you just asked is correct, and that you are on the right path. The Bible talks of this Spirit in John 14: 26, "But the Comforter, which is the Holy Ghost, whom the Father will send in my name, he shall teach you all things, and bring all things to your remembrance, whatsoever I have said unto you." The Spirit can also help us remember the truths we were once taught.

The Spirit can feel like the chills, a sudden feeling of happiness, or warmth in your chest. The Spirit can also feel like warm honey is being poured down from your head to your toes. You may feel like crying, or that the Earth's colors look brighter and you enjoy being outside more. You may suddenly get wonderful ideas for how to be better, or your understanding is enhanced or enlightened. You may start feeling stronger or more confident in your ability to conquer the dragon. Basically if it feels good, it's from God.

These are called the fruits of the Spirit. They confirm that God is communicating with you and that you are on the right path for your life. After discussing what the Spirit feels like, our Heavenly Father mentions that when you get an answer, remember that Satan will test you. Therefore, God encourages us when we get an answer or prompting, to follow it *immediately*. Satan will try to convince us that it wasn't from God and will try even harder after we get answers from God to thwart our new conviction to stay on the path.

The Spirit can be a constant guide throughout our lives. It is there to warn of us danger and confirm good choices. **As we embrace this gift of being guided in our lives, we will find a strength inside to stay true to our course and to our Heavenly Father's plan.**

After our Heavenly Father has explained and extended to us our gifts, talents, armor of God, light of Christ, and fruits of the spirit, He hugs us tightly and tells us about two more things: the Veil and Honor.

The Veil

Our Heavenly Father explains that the Veil is like memory loss. Our memories of the Preexistence are still there, but will be tucked deep down in our minds. We must prove to Heavenly Father we are worthy of a crown without knowing exactly the obstacles we will encounter. Having a veil over our minds teaches us to have faith and hope for things to come. Because of the Veil, we can rediscover that we once were warriors of light and truth in the preexistence. The veil also encourages us to seek truths we once knew, and to find faith again that God is our Father and that we are of royal birth.

Though the Veil hides our memories, God asks us to remember that He has a plan for us and we must have hope that we will be worthy to live with Him again through His son, Jesus Christ. He explains without the veil, our quest would be like walking in green pastures for only a mile with no bumps in the roads. Could we truly be tested on this Earthly quest if we knew every step to take? No. Therefore, the veil encourages us to reach out to God, to use His armor, to listen to the Spirit, to embrace the light, and ultimately to conquer through our own efforts using faith. For faith is believing things that cannot be seen, but are true.

Return with Honor

The last thing our Heavenly Father tells us before we begin our quest here on Earth is to return with honor. What does that mean exactly? Does it mean we have to be perfect on our quest? No. It means we must try and use all of the tools our Father has given us: gifts, talents, strengths, armor, light of Christ, and the Spirit to overcome Satan, while trying not to do too much damage to ourselves or others.

Returning with honor means we have fought a good fight and returned home victorious.

When all is said and done, our Heavenly Father wants to be proud of us and our actions for overcoming our trials and challenges while honestly trying to do our best. He knows we will get bruised and sometimes beaten (overcome). God just doesn't want us to dance with the Devil most of our life and then at the end think we can just repent (on our death bed), say we're sorry and feel we are worthy to receive our eternal reward as heirs. He understands that we will mess up many times in our lives. But He doesn't want us to abuse our free agency and hurt others deeply. Returning with honor is basically repenting for our wrongs, striving to do better, and being honest while doing it.

What righteous king would crown a prince or princess who wasted their quest to living it up in sin, revenge, murder, selfishness, and all other acts conceived by Satan? God wants us to give our best efforts and repent when we fall. He wants us to build character, find compassion, love the less fortunate, fight for the weak and humbly seek His guidance, so we can return with honor.

After our Heavenly Father's final counsel to each of us, He sends us on our way to begin our quest here on Earth. He tells us it is a quest that will never be matched. One with mists of darkness, dragons, deception, temptation, cliffs, uphill battles, scrapes, cuts, wounds, narrow paths, dark dungeons and evil lurking everywhere. Though Satan has planned well for trying to make us fail, God gave us what we would need to succeed: The armor of God, light of Christ, strengths, talents, gifts, the Spirit, prayer, family, and, ultimately, Jesus Christ our Savior.

Your Quest Begins

Your first quest is to gather proof that you are a child of God and that you are of royal birth. You can find this out by reading the scripture below, praying and noticing how you feel.

Remember in Romans 8:17 the Bible tells us, "And if children, then heirs; heirs of God, and joint-heirs with Christ. Ask God if this is true.

Your second quest is to write down how you feel about being an heir of God. Write down how it makes you feel to know you are a prince or princes of the Heavenly King. What does knowing this do for your confidence and self-esteem? Would you treat yourself better and make wise chooses if you knew you were royalty? Picture yourself as Royalty here on Earth, would your life be different? Why?

Your third quest is to ask God if Satan is real. Is he our enemy and the one we must conquer? Write down how knowing Satan is real will help you when temptation comes.

Will knowing that Satan wants you to fail make you want to succeed even more? What does knowing Satan wants to knock you off your potential throne and be as miserable as him do for you?

Your final quest is to ask if this quest is real, if you are on this Earth to be tested to prove yourself worthy as an heir in His Kingdom. Then write down how many pieces of the armor of God you are currently using. If you are not currently using many, commit to adding some in your life.

As we invite God in our life, and use the tools He has given, we will not only feel closer and more secure with Him, but stronger in defeating the dragon, Satan.

You are of royal birth

You did succeed in your first quest

You are strong enough to succeed in
your second quest here on Earth

The Quest for Knowledge

CHAPTER 2

The Quest for Knowledge

Discover why you are here

The Purpose of Life

Excitement filled the air as we were getting ready to leave the presence of our Heavenly Father, the King of Heaven and Earth, to begin our quest—a quest unmatched to anything we had been through thus far. This quest on Earth is for continued freedom of choice, for knowledge, for learning and growth, and, ultimately, to be heirs to the Kingdom of God.

As we are getting ready to leave, our Heavenly Father reminds us that once we are on Earth, we have two main reasons for being there. The first reason is to receive a physical body. The second is to be tested to see if we will do all that we can to prove ourselves worthy to return to our Heavenly Father as heirs in His Kingdom.

Physical body

All those who proved themselves worthy in their first test as Warriors of Light, fighting for the freedom of choice and being on the winning side, were each knighted with a body. The passing of our first estate is mentioned in Abr. 3:26, "And they who keep their first estate shall be added upon…"

This knighting of a body opened up a whole new world to us. For when we were spirits living with our Heavenly Father, we could only experience and feel so much. However, when we were knighted with a body, our feelings and experiences were enhanced a hundredfold. We could now feel and experience all emotions and temptations to their fullest. Being knighted with our bodies allowed us to feel more joy, happiness, love, pleasure, sensation and passion. But, it also allowed us to feel more sadness, hate, remorse, guilt, and shame than our spirits ever could.

Our bodies brought not only enhanced emotion, but new experiences of health, strength, and power, as well as the frailties of pain, illness, weakness and temptation. **Being knighted with a body because of our valiancy in the Preexistence was truly one of the ultimate rewards from our Father in Heaven,** as stated in 1 Cor. 6:19–20, "Know ye not that your body is the temple of the Holy Ghost which is in you, which ye have of God…" Our bodies are so special it is compared to God's temple.

Being knighted with the body is such a special gift from God. It is one that Satan and the other one-third of his followers will never receive. Since our bodies are a gift from God, God asks us to take special care of them. If you were given a new Lamborghini how would you treat this car? Would you take it four-wheeling, or write graffiti on it, or put water in it instead of gasoline? I dare say you wouldn't.

Well, our body should be treated with as much care and respect as you would the Lamborghini, one of the world's most expensive cars. For God views your body as one of His greatest creations and most expensive gifts. No other vessel could be used to go on such a difficult and taxing quest. Nor could you feel and experience all the emotions of joy, happiness, pleasure and pain without your body. Therefore, be kind to it. Be healthy. Take heed of what you put into it, what you write on it and what you fuel it with. Remember this is the only body you will ever be knighted with here on Earth.

To make this gift of our body last forever, our Heavenly Father, through His son, Jesus Christ, has made a way for us after we die to be restored to our physical body once again through resurrection. We will receive not a body that is bruised, broken, or missing limbs, but a body perfect, untouched, equally proportionate and potentially as radiant as the sun. All those who were knighted with a body will be restored to their body again after they die, as a gift for their valiancy in the Preexistence. Resurrection as a free gift is referenced in Acts 24:15, "…that there shall be a resurrection of the dead, both of the just and unjust."

Whether we make right choices or not, and whether we return home as a worthy heirs or not, once knighted with a body, this gift will never be taken away. Satan knows this. He is extremely angry that he will never receive a body, so beware. This dragon of lies and deception and bitterness will try to do everything in his power to have you destroy your gift through unhealthy habits, abusive actions and riotous living. This evil dragon will do anything he can to breathe out fire (temptations) in order to help you destroy your body here on Earth and, ultimately, to knock you off your potential throne.

Taking care of our body is part of our quest. The other part is to see what choices we will make when obstacles befall us while on our path home.

Free Agency – The Power of Choice

Remember, during the war in Heaven, we fought over free agency— not over receiving a physical body, but over the power to choose. Ask yourself: Why do you think we fought so valiantly to make our own choices and Satan, with his one-third, fought so valiantly to choose for us? It's because there is an energy created when we make choices. That energy produces a type of power inside each of us; it drives us to live and be free. Try and think of a time when you weren't given a choice because it was forced on you. Didn't you feel powerless in that moment? The reason you felt powerless and helpless is because the power of choosing for your life was given to another.

Satan still wants power over our choices. He will slowly and cunningly try to be the puppeteer in our lives through deceit, temptation and negative emotions. Therefore, when we choose what is wrong, we give our power away to Satan. When we choose what is right, we keep the power within ourselves. When we make choices—whether good or bad—those choices have the power to shape us into whom and what we will become.

Remember, you fought valiantly in the Preexistence for the freedom of choice. Will you do it again here? Will you keep the power within by cutting the strings of deception that Satan is trying to attach to your soul? Or, will you continue to ignore the fact that he has become your puppeteer because of the poor choices you have made? These poor choices have limited your freedom, just like being puppeted. This quest is yours. Only you have the power within to be successful.

All those who were knighted with a body (i.e., all humans on Earth) were also given free agency. The Lord describes free agency in Abr. 3:25, "And we will prove them herewith, to see if they will do all things whatsoever the Lord their God shall command them." Free agency is

simply the right to choose between right and wrong. Free agency enables us to make choices every day—whether big or small—that can impact our lives. Because of free agency, we have the option of choosing to use the armor of God, listen to the Spirit, counsel with our parents, make wise choices and stay true to our course. The choice is always ours. Remember, the freedom of choice is what we fought for in the Preexistence, will you continue to fight for it here?

Put on the Whole Armour of God in order to Quench Satan's Lies.

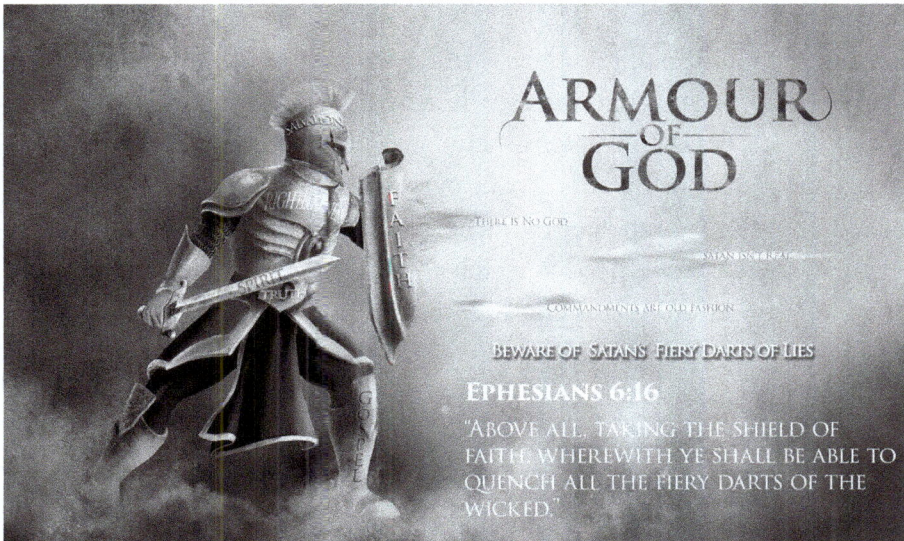

When we were placed on this Earth and sent on this quest, the war began again for Satan. It's a different war. This time we already have our free agency. However, Satan is still out there trying to do whatever he can to take it away from us through deception, temptation and confusion. When we fall into his trap, we are giving him our free agency and limiting our choices. For example, if you allow yourself to be trapped in a corner (because of poor choices) with the dragon facing you and watching every move, you'll find your choices have now become limited (i.e. jail, probation, addiction).

Throughout our quest, we will face obstacles, trials, challenges and darkness. These challenges will try to get in our way of completing our task. What is our task? Our task is simply to overcome the obstacles, trials, challenges, and mists of darkness by using our free agency, talents, gifts, strengths, armor, and the Spirit, so that we might come out victorious in the end.

So let's begin this quest with knowledge. Knowledge of how Satan does his thing and where he hides, and how Jesus Christ does His thing and is out in the open to help us.

Satan

Satan's plan and main purpose is to do whatever he can to help us destroy our bodies through misuse, destroy our minds through confusion and hopelessness, and destroy our happiness through anger, revenge and hate. Satan still wants power over our wills and choices. He tries subtly to be our puppeteer by using sin, anger and misuse of our free agency. Therefore, we need to watch carefully with both eyes open when making choices. Will this choice lead me closer to my goal of conquering this quest? Or will this choice allow Satan to be the puppeteer in my future decisions?

Picture this: You find yourself on your quest to return back to the castle, God's Kingdom, as an heir to the throne. As you see yourself struggling (addiction), not knowing what to do or what lies ahead, you feel discouraged and tired. You know, though you're exhausted, that you still must defeat this dragon (who makes you doubt your strength). God knows how you feel, as stated in Hebrews 12:1, "Wherefore seeing we also are compassed about with so great a cloud of witnesses, let us lay aside every weight, and the sin which doth so easily beset us, and let us run with patience the race that is set before us."

As you look ahead, you see the path that you must take (recovery). The path consists of some dark forests (doubt), rocky uphill climbs (withdrawals), and, at times, treacherous terrain (hard work). What do you do? Do you not even try?

Watch out for Satan's Fiery Darts of Lies!

You're NOT Strong Enough

Satan's plan is to discourage us by clouding our view of the strength that we have inside, the tools that we have readily available, and the knowledge that we have succeeded once before in conquering him. He wants us so badly to fail through not even trying. He hopes that we will forget that each of us has the strength to defeat this dragon. Remember, he is the Father of Lies and deception. So, beware of the mists of darkness, of despair and of hopelessness the angry dragon creates through the common mistakes that we all will make here on Earth. Though we may fall at times, we must still try. For every obstacle or negative feeling we encounter can be overcome with the tools the King gave us before we left.

The Savior Jesus Christ

Each of us knew when we fought for free agency that there would be opposition and opposites of everything we would experience here on Earth. We knew that where bad is, there is always good. Where there is confusion, there is always knowledge. Everything has its opposite: good and bad, evil and righteous, health and sickness, pleasure and pain. Similarly, the Savior Jesus Christ is the exact opposite of Satan, the dragon. So, during our quest, we may encounter many obstacles, trials, confusion, challenges and other things that bring darkness to our minds. But, our Heavenly Father—through His son Jesus Christ, our brother—created tools to overcome anything we might face, especially darkness. For the Savior, Jesus Christ, is the light of the world.

Jesus Christ is our strongest tool here on Earth. He went before us, paved the way and removed as many obstacles as He could (the resurrection), if Christ would not have been raised the third day after His death then none of us would be given our bodies back, and made perfect, after we die.

Jesus Christ also provided a way for us to get back on our path every time we fall off (the atonement). Jesus provided a way for us to climb back up, learn from our mistakes and move on. Only through Jesus Christ can humans complete their quest as stated in Acts 4:12, "…for there is none other name under heaven given among men, whereby we must be saved."

Jesus showed us the way when He went on the path first. He was bruised, beaten and spit upon and even nailed to the Cross, so that we may be given every opportunity to succeed. The difference between us and Jesus Christ is that He had to do it perfectly so that we wouldn't have to. All He asks is, when we fall down, or even fall off the cliff of life, that we ask Him to forgive us and help us get back on the path. Satan has his plans of deception to try to be our puppeteer in our lives. But, the Savior, Jesus Christ, has supplied the tools to cut to the strings, heal our wounds, and ultimately slay the dragon. Therefore remember, you are strong enough, with the Jesus Christ's help, to get past anything that falls along the path of your life.

Imagine, for a moment, going out to battle. When you think of a battle, would you think of green pastures, balloons, little children playing and having a good time? No. When people think of a battle, they think of war, bloodshed, fighting, tactics, leadership, ranks, and, hopefully, victories. This quest that we are on is a battle. A battle to win the war that Satan has created down here on Earth. Satan has created the Earth to be dark, dreary, violent, sinful and confusing.

Our Heavenly Father knew this before He sent us to Earth. He knew we would need whatever He could possibly give us (without taking away our free agency) to win this war. He, like a general, would not send out his troops (heirs to the Kingdom) to fight a war without the necessary protection to win it. With that said, I believe God not only gave us the strengths, talents, and gifts to overcome anything we would encounter, but He also took into account everything when deciding the trials we would face. I believe that before He sent out His princes and princesses on their quest, the King of the land, God, gave them knowledge of what they would face—or at least the big things they would face—on their quest. In other words, I believe each of us knew about and agreed to the trials we would face in order to prove ourselves worthy to live with God again.

Why would we agree to do that? Any good leader or general of an army prepares his troops for war the best that he can (trials) before sending them out. No general can prepare for everything they might encounter (challenges), but he can prepare them for the most obvious of what they would encounter (trials). Therefore, each of us was made strong enough for anything that we would and could encounter on our quest back home. In 1 Tim. 4:14, "Neglect not the gift that is in thee…" states we are given the gifts necessary to overcome trials and challenges.

Trials and Challenges

As heirs to the Kingdom of God, we must prove ourselves worthy to return home and claim our reward. To prove ourselves worthy we must be tested, though not all tests have to be surprises. As our Heavenly Father sent us on this quest, He equipped us with what we needed for the unique trials each of us must face to show Him we will still believe and want to come home.

What is a trial? A trial is something I believe we accepted in the Preexistence. It will help prove ourselves to God, make us stronger, build character and allow others to assist us on Earth (i.e., cancer, loss of a limb, chronic pain, fatherless, poor neighborhood…).

A challenge, on the other hand, is something that afflicts us due to our poor choices or the choices of others. (i.e., being raped, bullied, beaten, taking drugs, joining a gang…).

Trials are what we accepted in the Preexistence, while challenges are caused by free agency, though God uses both for our learning and growth. Our Heavenly Father will give us what we need, when we need it during each part of our quest. For example, if we get poisoned along the way, He will give us an antidote (atonement). If we get wounded along the way, He will teach us how to bandage it up (forgiveness). If we lose our way because the darkness that surrounds us, He will give us a huge flashlight to light the way (the light of Christ).

Trials

When each of us was placed on Earth to fulfill our quest, we came prepared with our own set of gifts, as stated in 1 Cor. 12:4, "Now there are diversities of gifts, but the same Spirit," for our own set of trials. When our Heavenly Father handpicked each of our trials for our learning and growth, He made sure we would also be equipped with what was needed: the strength, talents, and gifts to conquer and overcome any trial. Our trials can sometimes look like weakness, illness, mental problems, family problems, success, loneliness…For example, let's say, along your path you face needing to climb a vertical mountain (alcoholic parents). Do you doubt that God would have provided a harness, rope, and pitons in order to scale the mountain? God loves us and we are His children. Why wouldn't He?

When trials were handpicked for us, everything was taken into consideration: our strengths, what would really test us, what our limits were, and who would be helping us. Trials are given to test us to see if we will still believe, trust and love God. For example: Will a popular kid still need God? Will a bullied kid curse God? Will a sick kid hate God? Some would think being popular would not be a trial, but to some, it is. A trial is something that will test us to see if we will still love and counsel with God.

What obstacle are you facing right now and is it bringing you closer or farther away from God? Trials are here to test us and teach us certain lessons. The quest you are on may not be easy, or the trials that you are faced with might not be solved quickly. But each trial is specific to the person who's going through it.

Focus inward on what you need to overcome, and believe God has given you the strength to do so. Beware, though, of the dragon who is trying to consume you with his fiery darts of lies. For he will want you to think you can't overcome the trial placed before you or that the trial of others are easier and would be better for you. Satan wants us to lose our focus on our own path by being consumed by what others are doing on their path. Remember, each of us was sent on our own quest and given our own set a talents and strengths to overcome the obstacles that we would be faced with. Don't let confusion and envy cloud your view of what you must do in order to return home.

There may be times on your quest that you have to scale a mountain (stand up for your beliefs) to reach a higher plateau in your life. You may feel there is no way you could accomplish this. When you feel this way remember two things.

First, God promised that you will never have a challenge, temp-tation, or trial placed upon you that you cannot handle as stated in 1 Cor. 10:13, "...who will not suffer you to be tempted above that ye are able; but will with the temptation also make a way to escape, that ye may be able to bear it."

Second, before Heavenly Father sent us out on our own quest, God made sure we had every talent, strength, and gift we would need to overcome any trial or challenge that we would be faced with while on Earth. Our Heavenly Father knew that trials would test us and challenges befall us. But, He sent us prepared and He is confident we can conquer and return home.

My Quest for Knowledge

My quest for knowledge began thirteen years ago when I started having daily headaches. At first, my headaches were irritating at most. But then, over time, they got more and more severe. As the severity increased, my headaches started turning into migraines. Every migraine started off at the back of my head, came up and over behind my eye, causing my eye to be slightly blind, and then culminated in vomiting for two or three hours. This pattern of headaches every day, and migraines two or three times a week continued for thirteen years. The pain was so excruciating and exhausting that, at times, my feelings toward God started to go sour.

I prayed every day that my headaches would go away and that I'd be able to find someone to assist me in relieving this pain. But, alas, my headaches continued. I searched out every doctor, massage therapist, acupuncturist, chiropractor, and energy worker that I could find to rid myself of these headaches. But, nothing worked. Day after day, I'd wake up suffering, sometimes cursing God for this trial. I felt it was too hard for me to bear.

Then, one day, I asked my husband to give me a blessing. A blessing is given by someone who holds the priesthood of God and is inspired to tell you what God wants you to know in that moment. In this particular blessing, my husband said something that opened my eyes to my own quest. He said, "Kassi, our Heavenly Father wants you to know that He loves you very much and He understands the pain and suffering you have felt and are feeling at this time. He wants you to continue to call on Him for strength and comfort while going through this trial."

My husband paused, "Kassi, the trial of your headaches was handpicked for you. This was the only way God could test you to see if you would still believe and have faith in Him while going through so much pain. Be strong and faithful and God will help you any way He can while you are going through this trial."

After the blessing, I felt a sense of peace fill my soul. From that time forward, I have been able to handle my daily headaches with peace.

I know that I am on a quest. This is one of those obstacles that may continue to be on my path for the rest of my life. But, I also know God made me strong enough to overcome it. This trial was handpicked for me to see if I will continue to believe and press forward, having faith that God will not test me more than I can bear. If I make good choices, despite my trials, then the quest I am on will be rewarded.

Challenges

The trials we are faced with are handpicked for us for our ultimate growth and learning, whereas, the *challenges* that befall us are because of free agency. Challenges are caused by the poor choices humans make that affect us personally. For example: My headaches are a trial for me because it was not caused by mine or others' poor choices, whereas my parents' divorce was my challenge.

A challenge occurs when you or others caused you harm, and it affected your life deeply (raped). Some challenges are harder to overcome and take a lot more effort (forgiveness, healing, help, new beliefs…) on your part than others. But, God will make sure you will have what you need, when you need it. Remember, God cannot take away humans' free agency, but He can make us strong enough to get through anything we are challenged with.

When challenges come your way, know that God would not have ever sent us down here without the right tools to fix our problems or a way to find relief from them. This relief from our challenges is found in Matt. 11:28-30, which states, "Come unto me, all ye that labour and are heavy laden, and I will give you rest…"

Picture yourself on the path toward returning home as an heir to the throne. You have fought the dragon of lies, accepted your trial of your parents' divorce, feel secure with the progress you've made so far and are feeling pretty good about yourself. Then, as you're walking back, someone comes over and intentionally throws you to the ground (bullied). What you do?

This is a new challenge. Someone has abused their free agency and hurt you. Do you give up? Do you stop because someone else has lost sight of who they are and the quest they are supposed to be on? Or do you pick yourself up, dust yourself off, forgive them, and keep moving forward?

Throughout our lives we will encounter challenges because of other people. It is part of our quest to see what we will do with the challenges with which we are faced when other people use their free agency poorly.

Faith Strengthened by Knowledge

God gave everyone the strengths needed to overcome their personal problems and challenges. Now, it's our job to believe and have faith that He has given us what we need to overcome anything, so that we can succeed. If you have a trial or challenge that is extremely difficult, have the faith to ask for His help and it will be given to you. If you believe that you are strong enough for your trials, then use that knowledge to help you during your obstacles here on Earth.

There may be times when someone crosses your path and you can't handle the situation alone (i.e., child being molested). That's why God places others (like family) in your path to help you. Remember, God can help you overcome anything—no matter what life throws at you. With Him you are strong enough.

Ultimate strength to overcome anything comes
from believing and counseling with God.

The purpose of life, and the purpose of the quest, is to be challenged, to be tried and to be true to our course. Each quest we face will be full of obstacles, darkness, confusion, doubt and fear. Just remember, when we passed our first quest of being warriors for freedom and light and then were knighted with the body. We were thrilled to take part in this test to prove ourselves worthy to be heirs to the Kingdom of God. We were thrilled because we knew we had what it takes to overcome anything.

Anything worth having in this life, and in the next, will take hard work, struggle, mistakes and even falling down. **Never give up.** Never stop fighting, for you are worth the end reward. No matter what struggles or fights we will have with the dragon on our quest, just know that our Heavenly Father gave us every strength, talent, tool, pieces of armor, and insight that we would need to come out victorious in the end. Everyone is strong enough to return home with honor after defeating the dragon, Satan, and conquering their quest.

Your Quest for Knowledge

Your first quest is to be grateful for your body. I want you to take an hour and not use your legs. You can crawl if you need something. But, you cannot walk. You may think: *That's easy. I will just watch TV.* Then, instead, do not use your eyes. Take this challenge seriously.

Write down how limited you felt. What kind of struggle it was. And, hopefully, how grateful you are to have this tool (body) to enjoy life with.

Your second quest is to give your free agency away. For one hour, I want you to have everyone make all of your choices. This means needing to go the bathroom, eat, sleep, brush your teeth…every decision. You cannot choose anything for yourself. Find someone that will tell you what to do. (Maybe your younger sibling. They'd love that.)

How did you feel about not being able to choose for yourself? How is this like having Satan trying to take away our choices through coaxing us to misuse our free agency (i.e., you steal, you're in jail). Write down the similarities between these two experiences.

Your Last quest is to write down your trials (things, people that unintentionally inhibit you) and your challenges (caused by poor choices made by you or others). Now, write down the gifts and strengths you feel you have that will help you overcome. Then write down the ones you will need God's help with. Ask for His help.

Your body is a gift

Your free agency a reward

Your trials a character builder

Your Challenge is a testing ground

The Quest for Inner Strength

CHAPTER 3

The Quest for Inner Strength
Discover what tools and strengths you have

ere we are on Earth, trying to find our way in this dark and dreary world, while constantly fighting with the dragon. We have each been given this physical body and the freedom to choose. But now, we find ourselves searching for more because of our challenges and trials. We are searching for inner strength, deeper peace and feelings of greater love. We find ourselves looking for more than what the world can give. In other words, we find ourselves smack dab in the mists of darkness, trying to find the light that shows us our way back home.

Though we realize we are of royal birth, we still find ourselves asking questions like: *What do we do when we fall down? What do we do if the dark mists get too intense? How do we know what we should avoid on our paths?* Our Heavenly Father not only gave us the tools, the Spirit, family and the armor of God to help us on our quest, but He also gave us other ways of knowing what to avoid, where to turn for guidance and what to do when we fall.

Each of our Heavenly Father's children is unique in his/ her personality, purpose, quest, strengths and weaknesses.

Strengths and Weaknesses

When searching for inner strength, we must begin by looking in the mirror. Our Heavenly Father has given each of us strengths and weaknesses. Our strengths are here to build confidence in our ability to conquer in our individual quests. Our weaknesses are here to keep us humble and seek God's assistance and counsel.

To find inner strength, we must first discover our strengths and weaknesses. If we know our strengths and weaknesses, then we can be better prepared to know what we can handle and what we can't handle alone.

To find out what your strength and weaknesses are, you can do two things. First, you can find out by just asking someone you trust and cares about you. Second, you can search within.

Ask Someone Else

When you ask someone what they think your strengths and weaknesses are, you might find it a bit scary because you feel vulnerable. Therefore, you would want to ask someone who really knows you and cares about you. Ask this trusted person what strengths and talents they see you have inside. Then ask them what they see you need to be careful of (weaknesses). Gather this information. Then, look within. If you are satisfied with the answers, focus on those. If one or two don't seem to fit, then look deep inside and be honest with yourself. Ask yourself: *Are these characteristics really true?* If they aren't, toss them out. If they are and you didn't like how they made you feel, they are probably things you need to deal with, especially if your instinct was to toss them out quickly. After you've asked the opinion of a trusted person, you can leave it at that or you can try the second way: to search within.

Search within

When searching within, write down the things that you're good at—things that come easy to you (e.g., smart, good with kids, kind, forgiving). When you are thinking of things that you're good at, be kind to yourself. No one else has to see this list except for you. So, be proud of yourself. It's okay to know that you have talents and strengths from God. We all do. Our Heavenly Father gave everyone strengths, so that we can enjoy life and be happy.

List your strengths first when searching within, so that the weaknesses are easier to admit. Remember, our Heavenly Father gives us weaknesses so that we will draw close to Him and rely on Him. If all humans were good at everything and never had to work on anything, then this quest of ours would be easy.

As you think about your weaknesses, write down the things you have trouble with and could work on. For example: If you are quick to anger, then your temper is a weakness. If you are easily addicted to things (i.e., food, alcohol, drugs, pornography, women, gossip…), then self-control is a weakness.

Knowledge is Power

You may ask: *Why is knowing our strengths and weaknesses a powerful tool for inner strength?* Knowing what to watch out for (weaknesses) and what to use when your confidence is low (strengths) will not only help you on this quest, but will help you be smarter than the dragon. Knowledge is power. Your knowledge of your strengths and weaknesses will not only make you more powerful on your quest, but will also help you know what pitfalls to avoid.

If you know you have a problem with pornography, and you want to overcome it, wouldn't this knowledge give you power when choosing your unobserved activities? What would you do when no one is looking? Knowing our weaknesses and what to avoid will help us when those weaknesses are challenged. Knowing how to avoid certain pitfalls on our quest and what strengths to draw on when struggling will help us on this quest to becoming an heir in the Kingdom of God.

Drawing on our strengths will help build confidence, and being watchful when our weaknesses are challenged, will help us defeat the dragon when He tries to lure us in through temptation. Knowing each will make us stronger during our quest here on Earth. For instance, if you know you're not good at climbing, but you are really good at navigating, which activity will you choose when given the opportunity? Use your God given strengths to build your confidence and bring joy to your life.

Discovering our strengths and weaknesses is just the tip of the iceberg on finding inner strength. Though the strengths will aid us in doing well on our quest, what happens when we fall because of our weaknesses? Who can pick us up? Who's going to heal us when we get wounded? And who can help us fight the dragon? The one who can help us when we fall, when we get wounded, and when we need to destroy the dragon is the one who went before us. It is the one who finished His quest perfectly, so that we didn't have to. His name is Jesus Christ, our Savior.

Jesus Christ has many names. One is the Savior of the World. Another is the Healer, the Peacemaker, and the Sacrificial Lamb. Jesus Christ gets these names because of the quest that He had to finish. His ultimate and all-powerful quest was to die for the sins of the world and to be resurrected. As we mentioned before, resurrection is a free gift to all those who passed their first quest in the Preexistence. When He died for the sins of the world, Jesus did so for those who would seek His forgiveness, healing power, and comfort in this dreary world. As a result, we can draw inner strength knowing we can be healed when we get hurt and forgiven when we have fallen. The combination of His sacrifice and resurrection is called the atonement.

♥ Christ's Atonement

The atonement has three major purposes. The first purpose is to be forgiven for sin. (A sin is an act contrary to God's commandments that was done on purpose.) Jesus Christ suffered in Gethsemane for every human sin that could ever be done on this Earth. In Luke 22: 41 we read, "…Saying, Father, if thou be willing, remove this cup from me: nevertheless not my will, but thine, be done…" Though this suffering caused Him and the heavens to tremble because of pain, He still did the will of the Father, for us.

Jesus Christ suffered for the sins of the world so that, if we repent, we can be forgiven. When Jesus Christ suffered in Gethsemane, He felt every sin that would ever be conceived here on Earth so that, no matter what we do wrong, we can be forgiven. He did this so that, if we fall off our path—whether how small (a lie) or large (stealing)—we can be forgiven, picked up and put back on our path. No quest is over here on Earth, no matter how many times we fall, because of the atonement.

Christ suffered so that we did not have to lose our reward as heirs in the Kingdom of God if we messed up. Therefore, if you have sinned, no matter how great, and you repent, you have the opportunity of having it wiped away through the Savior's atonement. For example: Let's say, while trekking on your path, you find yourself in a bad mood and hungry. As you walk along, you come across another napping under a tree. As you look closer, you notice they left their food out in the open, so you help yourself. Later that day, you start to feel bad because you just stole someone else's food. You repent and ask God to truly forgive you. As God sees you are truly sorry, He forgives you and wipes that sin clean.

The second purpose of the atonement is to make up the difference between our mistakes (things done unintentionally) and God's perfection. In other words, the atonement makes up for the gap between God's perfection and our imperfections. In order to receive and be like our Heavenly Father, we must complete our task of defeating the dragon, following Christ's example and finishing our quest.

The only way to do this is to have Jesus Christ bridge the gap between the impossible task of doing everything perfectly and doing everything using our best efforts. For example: During your quest you come across a bridge full of planks that you must cross. You think to yourself, *No big deal*, so you proceed to cross. As you cross this unstable bridge, you find there are ten missing planks in front of you. What do you do? You can't go back because this is the only way home. So you pray for help. Because of the atonement, those ten planks are filled and you are able to cross. The atonement bridged the gap after you went as far as you could.

The third purpose of the atonement is to be healed. The atonement has the power to heal what has been done to you physically, sexually, emotionally, spiritually and mentally. It also has the power to heal illness, health problems, afflictions, hate, anger, revenge and spite. It is an all-encompassing, all-inclusive, all-powerful gift.

God and Jesus Christ knew that innocent people would be harmed by others—intentionally and unintentionally—here on Earth. They knew we needed a way to be healed on our quest when we got wounded. They knew there needed to be a way to be healed, not just for the sinner, but for the innocent.

The atonement has the power to heal; the power to bring back innocence when innocence was taken; to bring back faith where faith has been destroyed; to bring back health when sickness took over; to bring back trust when trust was abused; and to bring back wholeness to all empty souls. The atonement is readily available, just like the armor of God. The only way to use the benefit of the atonement, like the armor of God, is to seek and ask for it. As we use the atonement in our lives, we will not only find inner strength to keep going, but a sense of peace that Christ will make up the difference.

Prayer

To use the atonement, especially to its fullest, we must pray. Pray and ask God to heal us, forgive us and comfort us. The atonement does us no good if we do not pray and ask our Father to apply it. Therefore, we must learn to pray when seeking to use the atonement in our life and to get closer to God.

Prayer is the avenue that we need to use in order to communicate with our Heavenly Father. This communication can strengthen our spirits better than any other of God's tools.

> Our Heavenly Father did not leave us alone on our quest
> without a way for us to call Him when we need His help.

Prayer is the best way to light our path when we are struggling to find our way. Our Heavenly Father is the only one with the answers to all of our problems. Therefore, when you find yourself wondering aimlessly in the dark (divorced parents) on this tiny little path, who is the only one that can guide you through? When we pray and ask God to help us with our quest, we must do so having faith that He will answer. Remember, no other person on Earth will ever know you as well as God does. Therefore, it is wise to seek His counsel when looking for answers especially while in the dark.

If you have never prayed before, try it. Ask Him if He is there. This is an example on how to pray for those who are new to praying. But, remember, a prayer is simply any heartfelt communication between you and God. You'll want to call Him by name, (Dear Heavenly Father). Then, ask Him what you want to know. Basically, just talk to Him.

Once you are done talking with Him, end the prayer, "In the name of Jesus Christ, Amen." and then listen. Don't hang up. For example: If you were to call a friend, would you talk the whole time and then hang up before your friend had a chance to respond? Doubtful. The same thing applies to our Heavenly Father. We must wait for His response when asking for His help.

When you are done talking with God, see what comes to your mind or what you start to feel. The Spirit feels different to everyone. As mentioned in chapter one, the Spirit can sometimes feel like the chills. Perhaps, you'll start to cry. You might have some great ideas. Whatever you do feel, know that God is answering you and that He loves you.

The process of prayer is important. Equally important is what to do when receiving an answer to your prayers. When you do get a prompting or answer from God, follow it! If you don't, then why did you just pray? If we seek God's counsel through prayer and then do nothing with the answer He gives, it's like waiting all day to catch a fish then cutting the line when a fish is finally hooked. The answers from God are there to help you with your life and this quest. Make sure you act on the answers you receive.

Trust God's Opinion

One of Satan's greatest traps and deepest pitfalls is to convince us that God does not love us if He doesn't answer our prayers immediately.

Watch out for Satan's fiery Darts of Lies!

God doesn't love you

Our Heavenly Father does not answer prayers immediately for two reasons. First, if the thing we asked for is not good for us and we are asking God to approve it, He will not answer us. For example, if we are asking our Heavenly Father if we should go to our friend's party and our Heavenly Father knows at the party there's a group of kids putting date rape drugs in the drinks, He will not approve your request.

Our Heavenly Father is there to help us in achieving our quest, not to make it more difficult. He will never agree or confirm any answer that is not in your best interest. Therefore, it's important we trust our Heavenly Father's opinion. If He is not answering us or it feels wrong, trust Him for He knows everything and everyone. He will never lead us down dark alleys, only lighted streets.

The second reason our Heavenly Father will not answer prayers immediately is if it's not the right time. For example: We may feel we are ready to experience the world on our own and go on a trip to Europe. So we ask our Heavenly Father's opinion. Should we go? No response comes. What does that mean? Does it mean He doesn't want us to go? Not necessarily, it could just mean you're not ready. He may feel there's more for you to do in America and with your family before you go to Europe.

Timing is everything with our Heavenly Father. Let's say you are doing pretty well on your quest, and, as you are walking down this path, you come to a stream. As you near the stream, you see a boat. So you ask our Heavenly Father if you should cross the stream. And He doesn't answer. Now you're frustrated because you just want to get to the other side. So, you ask again. Still you get no answer. So you ask the third time and still no answer. Finally, you're tired of waiting. So, you get into the boat. As you are ready to push off from the shore, all of a sudden, a huge flash flood goes over the stream. Luckily, you were able to jump back onto dry land and be safe. Your Heavenly Father knew the flash flood was coming, so He didn't answer your prayer immediately. Once the flood was over, He then gave you the feeling to go ahead and go to the other side of the stream.

Prayers are answered when He feels the time is right and when He feels that what you're asking is good for you. Our Heavenly Father loves you very much and wants the best for you. So, trust Him when your answers don't come immediately. When Heavenly Father does answer your prayers, let Him guide you. The path He will take you on will be one of safety and peace. It will, ultimately, fulfill a successful quest.

Each one of us can achieve anything we want when we seek our Heavenly Father's guidance and counsel. Our Heavenly Father is the only one that can see through the darkness on our life's path. Counsel with Him. Ask His opinion. Most importantly, seek His guidance when you feel lost.

My Quest for Inner Strength

When I was thirteen years old and playing tennis in California, my mom moved down to be with me. The pressure she placed on me to succeed was overwhelming. It created a lot of tension between us. When my coach saw the pressure my mom was putting it on me, he said something to her. As a result, he was fired. Changing coaches and feeling the pressure of having to be a perfect tennis player dampened my desire to play well anymore. One day, when I was playing a couple of matches with this new coach and with my mom watching, I felt no desire to be there playing tennis. So, I lost every match.

After I was done playing, my mom and I got into the car to go home. Before starting the car, she turned to look at me, gave me a disgusted look and then started yelling at me. She told me she couldn't believe I had lost. She reminded me that she had moved to California so I could be a star. She couldn't understand why I would just lose so easily just because I didn't feel like playing anymore. After she was done venting her frustrations, she turned and hit me. She then told me to get out of the car and walk home. I got out of the car, thinking she just needed to cool down. But then, suddenly, she drove off leaving me there all alone.

Here I was, all by myself high up in the hills at nine o'clock at night. Most of the roads were covered with trees. There were no streetlights and only dirt paths to walk on. Our apartment was about a thirty-minute drive away and I didn't know how to get home because my mom had always driven me. I had no idea what to do. I was thirteen years old, in a tennis skirt, all by myself.

I was scared and lonely. All I could think of doing was to start praying and ask God to guide me home. After I prayed, I remembered a song I used to sing as a child in my church. The song was, "I am a child of God." The song talks about being one of the Heavenly Father's children and that, with Him, nothing is impossible. As I started to sing this song, I felt a peace come over me. Then, a feeling of happiness swept into my heart. I felt so happy in fact, that I started skipping. In about forty-five minutes I found myself in front of the apartment.

I was guided that day in the darkness of the night by a loving Heavenly Father who knew exactly how to help me get home.

Our Heavenly Father has sent us to this Earth to complete this quest with every tool that we will ever need to come out successfully. These tools and gifts will help us find inner strength. Strength comes from knowing, no matter what Satan tries to do to thwart our efforts, no matter what humans try to intentionally or unintentionally to push us off the path, we will always have what we need, when we need it, if we ask.

Our Heavenly Father hears our thoughts and knows our hearts. He knows when we are struggling and when we feel faint. Ask for His help through prayer. With His help we are always strong enough for any evil that gets in our way to make it back home.

Your Quest for Inner Strength

Your first quest for inner strength begins with discovering what strengths and weakness you have. You can either ask someone you know (as noted in the beginning of this chapter) or you can search within. Write down your strengths first and then your weaknesses.

Post your strengths on a wall and look at them every day, to help build confidence.

Once your strengths and weaknesses have been listed, write down how your strengths have helped you when you were struggling and how they can do so in the future. Then write down how your weaknesses have hindered your progress. Look within and make a plan for how you can be more aware when your weaknesses are challenged, so that you can avoid the pitfalls Satan will try and push you into. Try and be more conscious of the pitfalls that can easily grab you. Avoid them and ask God to turn your weaknesses into strengths.

Your second quest, after discovering your weaknesses and how they may have hindered your progress, take a look on where you are on your path. Have you been falling off just a little bit (lying, gossiping...), or by great heights (drugs, theft...)? Write down what you have done in your life that has knocked you off your path towards greatness. Then use the atonement of Christ to get back on the path and start fresh. In fact, start by recognizing you need the atonement to conquer Satan and his followers in order to make it back home.

There is power in acknowledging and accepting the fact that you need Jesus Christ to be happy and successful as an heir to the Kingdom of God. When we realize we need the Savior Jesus Christ, it helps us not stress over the little things we do wrong. Be open to your need for 's sacrifice to make it back home and write down what you need to repent for.

Your last quest is to learn to communicate with God. Pray and see if He is there. Ask Him if you have what it takes to make it back home. Prayer is something you can take with you anywhere in the world. Learn its power and how it guides you. Build a relationship again with your First Father. Talk to Him daily and ask for strength to overcome Satan.

You have been given strengths
to build confidence.

You have been given
weaknesses to stay humble.

You have been given the
Atonement to keep going.

You have been given
prayer to be guided.

The Quest for Answers

CHAPTER 4

The Quest for Answers
Discover why life is so hard

Knowing who you are and why you are here and how to fix your problems is a huge boost of strength for your quest. But, as you know, others are also on individual quests. Some of them may have lost their way and will be trying to knock you down or thwart your efforts to become an heir to the Kingdom of God. You may have realized that this quest is not easy. In fact, it can be very difficult. No doubt, you'd like some answers for why it is so hard.

Why Can Life Be So Hard?

We have trials and difficulties on our quest for three main reasons: First, so that we may learn to seek and follow the counsel of God, second, because of free agency. And third, the difficulty of the quest builds character and teaches us lessons.

First: Remember God

Ask yourself: Would you pray or need a higher power "God" if your quest was problem free? If your path had no obstacles, no people trying to push you off, or no dragon trying to destroy you, would you pray?

Maybe, maybe not. Having trials, challenges and Satan in our life encourages us to draw close and reach out to God.

If your quest is full of easy paths, blue skies and nice people would it be a real test? In order for a quest to do its job in proving our worthiness, it must have difficulty. Though this quest will be difficult, that doesn't mean that we can't conquer it. But to conquer it, we must reach out to the one who has done it before us and to the One that sees all and knows all, namely Jesus Christ and our Heavenly Father.

As we go through difficult times, we need to learn to love and have faith in our Heavenly Father—no matter what happens on our path. We need to believe that our Heavenly Father is watching out for us and will assist us every time we ask. Trials and challenges are there to draw us close to our Heavenly Father. He wants us to call on Him for help, understand and use the atonement of Christ, and seek His guidance and counsel so that we can achieve our goal and live with Him again.

Second: Free agency

Free agency is the biggest reason why our quest is fraught with difficulties. Though free agency is what we fought for in the Preexistence and was given to everyone as a gift, it can sometimes put quite a damper on our quest, sometimes because of us, and sometimes because of others. There is power when making choices, but sometimes this power can be abused.

It hurts our Heavenly Father to watch His children harm each other. But, He cannot take away anyone's free agency. If He were to take away our free agency and force us nor others to do what is right, then He would be following Satan's plan and cease to be God. Our Heavenly Father understands the quest can be difficult when we make poor choices or when others abuse their free agency and it affects us. But, God promised if we conquer our quest, despite what happens to us, we will be rewarded.

God is a loving and just God. Therefore, those that abuse their free agency and hurt you will have justice served to them—either here in this life or in the next. Please understand that, though God cannot take away the free agency of man and though He will make sure justice is served to those who abuse it, He has given us everything we need to overcome anything. When we mess up because we abuse our free agency, the atonement can wipe it clean. When others mess up and hurt us because of their free agency, the atonement can heal us.

So many have asked why bad things happen to good people. Most often it is because of the misuse of free agency. But God is a wise God, when we get hurt by others, He will use our trials and challenges for learning and growth. And because God is a just God, His justice system will punish those who abuse their free agency. Let's say you're being bullied at school. God cannot take away the free agency of the bully, but He can make you strong enough to endure what you're going through, brave enough to tell someone about it and smart enough to learn from this experience. Furthermore, if the bully does not repent, our Heavenly Father will make sure he pays for what he did to you in the next life.

Though others have their free agency to hurt you, you have the free agency to choose whether what has happened to you will destroy your life or make you stronger. We always have a choice on how to act when others' behavior affects us badly.

Free agency not only brings difficulty when people abuse it, but it brings opportunity for us to prove to our Heavenly Father that, no matter what happens to us here on Earth, we will achieve this quest. Every king or queen has hard choices to make when others in their land are making poor choices or trying to depose them. Similarly, this quest is to prepare us for our eternal reward as heirs in the Kingdom of God. We will need to learn how to act when others choose unwisely.

With your power to choose, you are strong enough
and gifted enough to act wisely and choose how
your trials and challenges will affect you.

Some of the acts done to you by others abusing their free agency have probably really gotten you down. Remember, God would not have sent you here on Earth if He didn't believe you could overcome anything with His help. If you are at the point where your feel like you're losing your grip while scaling a mountain (difficult trials) trying to reach better heights, extend your hand and ask God to help you. Our Heavenly Father will do everything in His power to help you without intruding on your free agency or that of others. **Trust Him and believe that He has your best interest at heart.**

Our Heavenly Father is very aware of the pain that we can feel because of our poor choices or the poor choices of others. This is why He is placed so many tools on Earth to assist us. One of them is the shield of faith. Faith that God will deal justly with those that harm us and faith that we are strong enough to climb any mountain placed before us. It is essential we have faith that God knows what we are going through when we are hurt and that He will send us exactly what we need when we ask.

God has made sure that we have people around us that can help us when we are struggling. He has made sure that we are strong enough, especially with His help, to get through anything. With that said, be careful where you place the blame when bad things happen to you, for your view could be clouded and darkened.

Blame game

One of Satan's biggest tools to thwart our divine nature and individual quests is to convince us to play the blame game. Satan wants us to blame God for all the bad that happens in this world. He wants us to blame God for others hurting us when they chose to abuse their free agency. Remember, God cannot take away the free agency of any human—no matter how evil that person is.

Watch out for Satan's Fiery Darts of Lies!

It's God's fault

If Satan succeeds in convincing us to blame God for the choices of humans, He may also convince us to take God out of the picture. If we take God out of the picture, then what happens to our quest, our divine nature and our individual worth? Those will also be tossed out. The day that that happens, we truly will be wandering aimlessly in a dark world.

Let God's actions be accounted unto God, and man's actions be the responsibility of man. Do not blame God for what man has done. Every human on Earth has the freedom to choose to be good or bad. Don't let Satan convince you to blame God, so you won't counsel with Him, seek His guidance and continue your quest.

If you find yourself deeply discouraged because of the actions of others, pray and ask our Heavenly Father for help. Ask Him to heal you and help you overcome the bad that has happened to you. Don't get stuck in the blame game. If you do, you will never find a solution to your problems. Though God can't take away man's free agency, He can help us through with the tools He has given us, through the healing power of the atonement and through helping us to try and learn from our trials and challenges.

3rd: Build Character and learn lessons

The things that happen to us on our quest will always be the product of free agency—our free agency and the free agency of others. Typically, when good things happen to us, we don't question it. But, when bad things happen to us, we question. Therefore, our Heavenly Father does not want us to just let go when things go wrong in our life. He wants us to learn from it. The trials you face here on Earth are for your learning and growth. They are the obstacles on the course that we must conquer.

Trials are uniquely chosen for us for our ultimate growth. Challenges are caused by others' poor choices. Our Heavenly Father wants us to learn and grow from both. You have unique strengths and gifts to overcome and learn the lessons that God wants you to learn. Others may encounter similar trials, but they aren't you and they won't learn the same lesson you do.

For example: Let's say two of your friends have been date raped by the same guy. (He went to jail.) One learned, over time, to forgive and move on. The other learned to forgive as well, but decided to make sure it didn't happen to others. So, she started a website to educate women on what to look for when dating. Each moved on, but ended up learning different lessons.

Each trial and challenge is unique to us and so are the lessons. Everyone will learn something different from their past experiences, though their experiences could be similar. Don't compare yourself to others when it comes to learning and growth. Each person learns and grows at a different speed, and with different lessons learned.

When looking at your past and discovering what you have learned from experiences in your life, please remember one thing: Your past is there for you to learn from, not dwell upon. Our past experiences are there to build character and teach us lessons. Our past is not there to be dwelt upon or consume us. If you dwell on your past and the negative things that have happened to you, you will find yourself stuck and unable to move forward.

Look at your past experiences and see how you can learn from them so you can move forward with your quest. For example, if you come across a berry bush on your path and you decide to eat this fruit, which results in making you sick, wouldn't you stay away from this type of berry next time? Similarly, God wants us to learn from our mistakes, trials and challenges, so as to make us wiser for the next obstacle during our quest.

No trial or challenge is wasted with God. Whether it's our own trials or the challenges that come from the choices of others, God can use them to our benefit if we allow Him. You have all the power to choose what to do with your experiences and challenges. Ask yourself next time a trial comes along: *Do I learn from this or do I allow it to cloud my view of God and myself?*

Same Lesson, Different Time

I encourage you to ask our Heavenly Father to make you stronger and build character because of your trials. If you find yourself always asking, "Why me?" instead of "What can I learn from this?" you will remain stuck. The "Why me?" question, will keep you walking in a circle on your quest and you will find you end up in the same place you started with no progress. The problem will continue to show up in your life. Let's say you find yourself dating the same type of abusive guy, over and over again and you have no idea why. It is because you have not learned to recognize an abusive guy or you believe you are not worthy of anything better.

If you find yourself facing the same problem over and over again, your problem will never go away until you take it on, overcome it and learn from it. Life's problems go away, or are easier to accept, when we learn the lesson. Our trials are for our learning and growth. They are the best way God could test us, to see if we would choose Him and be worthy as heirs in His Kingdom.

It is important you use your strengths and talents and prayers to overcome the obstacles that you are facing, so they won't repeat themselves. Let the lessons of life build character in you, so you can become stronger for the next trial that God has in store for you. God uses our trials as building blocks to better things, like becoming heirs in His Kingdom. Remember, your trials were handpicked for you, for your ultimate learning and growth. They are something you accepted in the Preexistence.

Perspective on Your Acceptance

It may be hard for you to believe that you may have agreed in the Preexistence to have these trials in your life. If you knew you did, wouldn't that give you the power to change, accept and be happy in this life no matter what? Changing your perspective on your family, trials, challenges and weaknesses can assist you in becoming more powerful about the way you handle them.

Let's say you had a dream of your future wife and you knew the dream was going to come true. Wouldn't that give you the confidence when you did finally meet her, for you to win her heart?

The concept is the same. If we knew we accepted our trials before we came to Earth and that God gave us what we would need to overcome these trials, wouldn't that give you the strength and confidence to achieve your quest no matter what?

Look at every challenge as a stepping-stone. View trials as things you can learn from and a reason to draw closer to your God. Let's say while you were in the Preexistence you were watching others go through their obstacle course on Earth. You saw someone climbing a mountain. As you watched this person climb (i.e., cancer), you knew that you could do the same mountain. You knew that type of trial was something you had the strength and courage to handle.

Now if you were to believe that you could scale a mountain, overcome cancer, wouldn't that give you the confidence to accomplish that task here on Earth?

By believing we can accomplish the things that are placed before us, we have won half the battle. Our belief will serve as power to defeat the dragon who tries to get in our way. If you can change your perspective and accept that you chose these trials, how much more confident and powerful would you be in your own life? If you can change your perspective, you are able to change how you overcome things.

Trials themselves do not define you. What defines you is how you act in those circumstances you are confronted with. If you can change your perspective about your trials, then they will become easier to learn from and overcome. Next time a trial or challenge comes along your path, step back and try to look at it as if you already conquered it. Perspective brings power and power brings success.

Be strong. Be prayerful. Use your talents, strengths, armour of God and perspective to overcome any obstacle on your quest.

ARMOUR OF GOD

EPHESIANS 6:11

"PUT ON THE WHOLE ARMOUR OF GOD, THAT YE MAY BE ABLE TO STAND AGAINST THE WILES OF THE DEVIL."

Our Heavenly Father is wise and all-powerful. He knows when your trials are too much for you to handle alone. Therefore, He can provide assistance by sending you another human to help you or by sending you a miracle. Miracles are still performed every day for the benefit and use of man.

♥ Miracles

The story I shared in the preface was full of miracles. The only way I could have succeeded on my quest to live with my father was by divine intervention. Miracles are happening all around us. Though we each have the strength to overcome our own trials, God can and will perform miracles as we need them. A miracle is an event attributed to divine intervention, an act that can't be explained, or something that was done so perfectly it could have come only from God.

Miracles, big or small, come for different reasons. God performs miracles for the human race, through those He has called to bring about His work and teachings (i.e., His gospel). Miracles also come through inspiration for the advancement of man (i.e., penicillin). And miracles can come to those who are trying to do what is right and need divine intervention.

Miracles are needed now more than ever because of the world in which we live. The quest that we must go through in the twenty-first century has more dark mists, a stronger dragon, tougher strings to cut through, harder terrain and confusing roadmaps. Satan is gaining more control over people through their poor choices now than ever before. He is the puppeteer to many people because of pornography, alcohol, drugs, etc. As a result, many people are letting Satan help dictate their choices, abusing their free agency and hurting others deeply.

Abuse

Abuse to children and the youth is more prevalent now than ever before. Miracles are needed now more than ever—especially for those who feel they are not strong enough to overcome the abuse that is happening to them.

If you are being abused by family, extended family (i.e., stepparents or stepsiblings), or by others, you need to speak up. No one deserves to be touched inappropriately, beaten physically, or spoke to cruelly. I want to share with you how Jesus Christ feels about the youth being abused. He states in Matt.18:6, "But who so shall offend one of these little ones which believe in me, it were better for him that a millstone were hanged about his neck, and that he were drowned in the depth of the sea." In another words, whoever harms one of His little children, it would be better for them never to have been born.

If Jesus Christ feels so strongly about people abusing others, let that give you strength to act in your best interest. **Be strong and brave. Tell someone if you are being abused.** Reach out to someone you can trust and tell them what's going on. You will never receive the help you deserve if you do not open your mouth and talk about the abuse. Do not be afraid. Ask our Heavenly Father for a miracle to help you get out of the abusive situation.

Our Heavenly Father will assist you and send you a miracle when the time is right if you ask. He loves you very much. It hurts Him deeply when His children misuse their agency and harm each other. **Do not let Satan convince you that God has deserted you.** Pray and do your part in finding relief from this abuse by finding someone that can help you. You are strong enough. Believe in yourself and save yourself from future pain by speaking up today.

I hope your quest for answers has been quenched. Each of us was given the gift of free agency. Not all will use it wisely. You can choose how you will act or react if others use their free agency towards you poorly. You have been given the strength, tools and opportunities to learn and grow from any challenge or trial that comes your way. Change your perspective on your trials and be confident that, with the help of our Heavenly Father, you can overcome anything, so that you may return home and receive your reward.

Your Quest for Answers

Start on your quest for answers by writing down how grateful you are to have free agency. Think of a time you were forced to do something. How did that make you feel? Then write down the good choices you've made and how you felt after you made them.

Your second quest is to write down the trials and challenges you have been faced with. Are they drawing you closer or farther away from God? If they are drawing you farther away, why? Do you blame God for the choices others have made that hurt you? If so, I encourage you to stop blaming God and start asking Him to help you. Ask Jesus Christ to begin healing you.

Then write down the trials you have overcome and post that some-where you can read it everyday. This will give you strength when you feel discouraged.

Your third quest is to write down what you have learned from your past experiences and how they made you stronger. Then write down those experiences in your past that you are still dwelling on. Think about how you can learn from them, so you can move on.

Your last quest for answers is for those of you who are being abused. Write down the names of those in your life that could help you get out of the abusive situation. Then I want you to pray for a miracle and go talk with one of them today.

You are strong enough for your trials.

God cannot take away mans' free agency.

You have the power to choose with perspective.

Miracles have not ceased.

The Quest for Freedom & Healing

CHAPTER 5

The Quest for Freedom & Healing
Discover the power of forgiveness

What does the quest for freedom involve? Don't we have our freedom to choose? You *do* have the freedom to choose, and so do others who might unintentionally or intentionally hurt you. The freedom I am referring to is from the darkness that clouds our minds when we don't forgive someone who has hurt us.

Our Heavenly Father cannot take away anyone's free agency, even those that hurt you. But He can give you a way to free yourself from the anger, hurt, and hopelessness.

The all-powerful gift that can heal you when others have wounded you is forgiveness. The power of forgiveness can change everything. It can change your outlook on your future, your feelings about the present and your perspective on the past. When you forgive someone for their actions that caused you harm, you are given the power to melt away all of your negative feelings toward them (i.e., anger, resentment, hurt, abandonment, hate, revenge.)

Have you ever been angry at someone and they had no idea you were mad at them? And that anger built up inside you, but it was not affecting the other person in the slightest. Or let me bring it closer to home. Let's say you're angry at your father for leaving the family. Whom is that anger destroying? For whom is the anger building up day after day until it is all-consuming? You. The dad, especially if he doesn't know you're mad at him for leaving, is probably unaffected by his hurtful actions.

Unforgiveness hurts and affects the one feeling it the most. You may want to believe that being angry at someone because they hurt you will hurt them somehow. It doesn't usually work that way. The negative feelings and emotions that come from unforgiveness will always affect you more than it could ever affect another.

Unforgiveness

Being unforgiving in your life could do more damage to you now and in the future than any other act could. How? Unforgiveness is the underlining root to many, if not all, negative thoughts, feelings and emotions. Bad things happen to each of us at some point. Those who do not forgive the person that harmed them will find that the aftermath of negative emotions bring more darkness then the act itself could.

When we allow unforgiveness to create dark mists (anger, hate) on our path home, we are giving Satan permission to help dictate our choices about what we will do with these negative feelings and emotions. For example, while walking along your path you come across another who hurts you deeply (rape). As you allow unforgiveness to consume your thoughts, feelings and emotions, you convince yourself to rebel against those who are just trying to help you tackle this vertical mountain. As a result of trying to scale this mountain alone, while the anger is blinding you, you fall. As a result, this unforgiveness brought negative feelings and results that ultimately caused you more harm.

Another example, if you are really angry because your parents got a divorce and you feel you have every right to rebel against them and become reckless with your life, who is that hurting? If you are participating in illegal activities because of your rebellion and you get caught, who goes to jail? It's not your parents. It's you. On the other hand, if you were to forgive your parents for their poor choices and learn from their mistakes, you would be free to have whatever life you wanted. Forgiveness brings freedom—not just freedom from the present negative emotions and feelings, but the freedom from Satan trying to be your puppeteer in your life because of negative circumstances.

Watch out for Satan's Fiery Darts of Lies!

Forgiveness is for the weak, Revenge is for the strong

Another type of reaction that is caused by not forgiving another's harmful act is revenge. Let's say you have been hurt deeply by someone in your life and because of all the negative thoughts and feelings that consume your life at the moment, Satan convinces you to seek revenge. The day you decide that revenge is your best course of action against the one who has hurt you is the day you become a puppet in the hands of Satan. And when Satan becomes your puppeteer, he not only will help you destroy your life, but the other persons' life as well. As a result, he will have destroyed two people's quests for the price of one.

It is important to be freed from unforgiveness in order to conquer your quest successfully. You may be asking, what about the one who raped me or beat me up or got me addicted to Meth. Must I still forgive them? Absolutely. After you have reported these illegal activities to the authorities, it is absolutely necessary for you to forgive them and let the law of the land claim its justice. Failing that, let God's justice do it's claiming. If we do not forgive those who have harmed us, then our hearts and minds will be filled with anger, hate, revenge and hopelessness. It could consume us and darken our path back home.

Unforgiveness produces negative and unproductive thoughts that can, and will, cause our hearts to be filled with hate, resentment and anger that can consume us. Such negative feelings will affect our current relationships, how we view the world and, ultimately, our life.

Let's say you find yourself not liking men, or you don't trust them, but you have no idea why. Ask yourself: Are you currently angry at your father? Are you resentful he left the family? Did he hurt your mother? Have you forgiven him yet? Unforgiveness will always spew out into other areas of our lives as it creates a dark mist on our path home. Satan will try to convince us that anger towards another, like our father, will not affect other areas in our life. Therefore, you may not think holding a grudge against your father is a big deal. But judging by the results of not trusting men, now maybe it is.

It is very important to forgive everyone who has hurt us. **Unforgiveness will become like a noxious weed that can take over other beautiful things in our life (i.e., close relationships).** Distressed relationships are just the beginning of what unforgiveness can do in our lives. It also has a way of clouding our view of reality. The reality is that our pain will never go away until we forgive.

Who's in Control?

When we let unforgiveness create darkness on our path home, it can greatly thwart our efforts of being successful on our quest. As a result, we let Satan and others control our future. Another's actions have the potential to stop our progress. Let's say you've been hurt deeply (i.e., -beaten), and you won't let it go by forgiving the abuser. Who's in control?

The abuser is in control. If you do not forgive the one who has harmed you, anger can take over your life. It can control you, you thoughts, your feelings, your outlook and, ultimately, your life. Do you want to give that power to the abuser again by reliving the experience and not forgiving him/her? When we don't forgive others for their harmful actions, we are giving our power to Satan and the person who harmed us. The choice is yours. **Do you want Satan in control of your life through unforgiveness?**

Resentment, anger, and hate caused by unforgiveness can create dark mists on our path home. Those dark mists can lead us to self-destructive paths. As a result of the darkness, some will try to do what they can to mask the pain from unforgiveness. These masks may look like drugs, alcohol, porn, suicide and premarital sex. Don't be fooled by Satan. He will have you believe that these acts will make the pain go away. They won't. They only make the pain worse by giving our future to Satan through following his path.

Heb. 4:12, "For the word of God is quick, and powerful, and sharper than any two edged sword."

Use the Sword of the Spirit to cut through the lies Satan is telling you. The Spirit can, and will, teach you what is right and wrong for your life. As a result, the Spirit can help you heal from the pain you are going through by keeping the power of choice with you.

Anytime Satan tries to be your puppeteer through anger, fear and hate, remember to use the truths you know to be true (i.e., love, forgiveness, and peace) to cut through the strings Satan tries to attach to your soul.

Forgiveness will lead to healing. Healing will save you on your quest back home. Forgiveness is the key to ridding ourselves of darkness on our path and remaining strong for future obstacle courses. The Lord believes forgiveness is so important to our well being that He made it a commandment, as explained in Matt 18:21-22, "Then came Peter to him, and said, 'Lord, how oft shall my brother sin against me, and I forgive him? till seven times?'

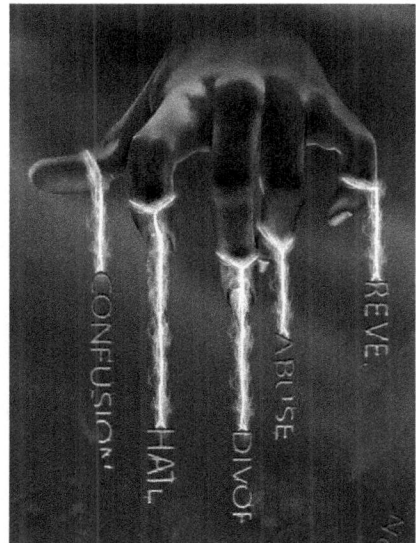

22. Jesus saith unto him, 'I say not unto thee, Until seven times: but, Until seventy times seven.' " Why do you think it's a commandment from God? Because this commandment is for **us,** not the other person. God knows unforgiveness will cloud our view and tempt us to go off course. Whereas forgiveness will bring us clear skies, stronger muscles and sharper vision on our quest back home.

Forgiveness and Healing

To explain how necessary forgiveness is on our quest back home, I want to use being wounded on our journey as an example. Picture, for a moment, being on this quest. On the path you are taking, you see trees on both sides. The terrain a bit rough (divorced parents), but nothing you can't handle. And as you're walking along enjoying life, someone jumps out of nowhere and stabs you in the leg (molested). He then takes off and leaves you there bleeding in pain. What you do?

The Band-Aid of Time

If you choose forgiveness, your first step is to put a Band-Aid on the wound. A Band-Aid represents time. Time is a necessary step when we have been wounded by others. It takes time to learn to forgive, to get our negative thoughts and feelings under control, to seek counsel when needed and to view things with more clarity then we would've the moment we were stabbed. In time, you will notice the Band-Aid of time did its job to stop the bleeding (i.e., anger, hurt, pain). But forgiveness starts when the Band-Aid is taken off and air is allowed to work its magic on the wound. This step is hard. The act of taking off the Band-Aid might be as painful as the wound itself (forgiveness can sometimes be very difficult).

The Air of Prayer

Air heals any wound completely. Without this step, the wound would remain moist and susceptible to infection. Prayer, like air, is a necessary step in complete forgiveness. As you start to forgive those that have harmed you, you'll find it easier to forgive them if you pray for them. Ask our Heavenly Father to help you forgive them. You will find, as you pray for those who hurt you, God can and will transform all the negative feelings you have towards them. As you pray for them, God can help you turn anger into compassion, hate to pity, revenge to charity and infection into healing.

The Scab of Forgiveness

After you've use the Band-Aid of time and the air of prayer, you will find the scab of forgiveness is in the final phase of healing. When a scab forms, it creates a hard shell over the wound, protecting it against future infection and bleeding. Similarly, forgiveness and prayer protects the one harmed against the infection of anger, revenge and despair. When we truly forgive another, the scab will fall off, allowing all the other negative feelings to fall off with it. You will find peace has replaced anger, compassion has replaced hate, and pity has replaced revenge. Only when you have completely forgiven someone will you ever be free from future infection.

The Scar of Accomplishment

You may find once the scab has fallen off there remains a scar. Do not look at this as being a bad thing. The scar is there to remind us of our accomplishment in forgiving that person and teaching us a valuable lesson. If your injury was due to carelessness (not heeding warning feelings), every time you look at the scar, you will be reminded to be more conscience of any warning feelings that come next time. As you learn to use the scars of accomplishments as valuable lessons, you will find peace faster because you are wiser now.

Infection

If you dwell (unforgiveness) on what happened to you (pick at the scab), you never achieve complete healing. Instead, you find an open sore that will irritate you for your entire quest. In fact, if the wound becomes infected with anger, hate and revenge, you will suffer more pain than the act itself (i.e. being raped, and then have it consume your entire life). If you do not bandage your stab wound and still try to continue your quest home, how far do you really feel you will make it before bleeding to death?

Be careful how far you take unforgiveness. It has the potential of doing more harm than the act itself (destroy your life by bleeding to death). If you find yourself not being able to stop the bleeding (anger) on your own and need help taking off the Band-Aid (forgiving), go and find a doctor (i.e., parents, family members, friends, teachers, peers, a therapist). Allow them to help you find the healing you deserve. It will become very difficult, if not impossible, to make it home if we do not bandage our wounds with forgiveness.

Forgiveness can unleash the power to heal—no matter what has happened to you on your life's quest. Forgiveness can mend all broken things: broken homes, broken relationships, broken hearts, broken hopes, broken trust and broken mirror (you).

Forgiveness and Communication

Prayer

Forgiveness is not always easy. Actually, most the time, it can be very difficult. Some of you may have had some very horrible experiences happen to you. Such experiences could make you feel entitled to be really angry and behave badly—especially if there was abuse involved. Such acts that seem unforgivable and still cause pain will require help from our Heavenly Father and His Son, Jesus Christ.

Our Heavenly Father gave man their free agency. But, He didn't give it to us to abuse it. The act of forgiving those who abuse it begins with utilizing Jesus Christ's act and healing power of the atonement. As we forgive those who have harmed us, it's also necessary to pray and ask our Heavenly Father to heal us. Christ's atonement can heal all wounds, no matter the severity. But, we must pray and ask for His healing balm.

For example, it is necessary when we have become wounded deeply, like being stabbed, to either put ointment on the wound or take some antibacterial medicine to ensure complete healing. The act of putting on Band-Aids to our wounds, taking them off, allowing them to scab over, and resulting in a scar is up to us. But the one that has the healing ointment or medicine is Jesus Christ. He can ensure complete healing to any wound we receive during our quest through the atonement. Jesus Christ is our ultimate doctor.

Communication with Others

It is not only extremely important to communicate with God when you have been wounded or things go wrong in your life, but it's also necessary to communicate with others if we have been harmed or are in need of help. It can be difficult, and sometimes a bit scary, to talk with another person when we have been harmed. We may feel, somehow, it's our fault and that we will get into trouble. Perhaps, we don't want to relive the experience by talking about it.

If you want to begin the forgiving process, you must communicate with someone when harm has been done to you—especially if it is a deep wound (i.e., abuse, beaten, verbally cruel...). If you cannot start talking about what has happened to you, then the wound will forever be susceptible to infection and take you off your course. Healing begins by getting it off your chest through communication. It's important to note when communicating, if your wound is deep, talk to someone who can help you. If the wound is small, try talking with the person who hurt you (gossip can be more damaging to you and the other person than keeping it inside).

Abuse and Secrets

Communication is vital if there's abuse involved. If you are keeping secrets of a harmful nature, no matter the reason, it will destroy you and possibly others. For example, if you been molested by an uncle and don't tell anyone, that same uncle could be molesting other people in your family. Keeping harmful secrets is never in your best interest. It can do severe damage to you and others.

Keeping secrets about abuse will not only lead to unforgiveness, but it will also start to control your life, dictate the choices you make and eventually mold your future. Do you really want what happened to you to control the rest of your life? If the abuse is not communicated to someone who can help you, you'll find it almost impossible to forgive the perpetrator. And if you can't find a way to forgive him/her, then that person who harmed you will have won Satan a victory or will keep you off your path back home. The event will consume your thoughts, feelings and, ultimately, your quest.

Seek help from others to overcome the negative feelings that are taking over your life. If you are being bullied, molested, beaten, or any other act that is consuming your thoughts with depression, violence, suicide, talk with someone. How will others know to help you if you don't open your mouth? Say something to an adult you can trust. Start talking to someone today so you can take back control of your life.

STAY in control of your life.
Stop the control they have over you,
Tell someone the secrets that are destroying you,
Act now to save others from the same fate,
Yield to the power of forgiveness.

Forgiveness and Parents

Filter and Forgive

Everyone has parents, and most kids seem to think their parents should be perfect. Parents are trying to survive themselves in this dark and dreary world while on their own quest. They were not given instructions on what to do when you make mistakes, when to ask for forgiveness when they have made mistakes, or what to do when problems arise. Therefore, let them be accountable for their own choices. Forgive them and be accountable for your own mistakes.

My Quest for Freedom

When I was growing up, my mom was so hurt and angry at my father for divorcing her that, when he came down to visit us every six weeks, my mom would tell us how evil he was, call him all sorts of names and beg us not to go. My mom was emotionally blind to everyone and everything around her. She was so swallowed up in her own pain that she couldn't emotionally see what she was doing to us kids by badmouthing our father.

There were times when she would say to us, "I can't believe that you are choosing to go with him. You are betraying me." At first, my mom's constant badmouthing of my father affected me. But, after a while, I learned that it was her hurt feelings talking and it had nothing to do with me. I would remind myself that those feelings were her feelings and not mine.

After taking a step back, I was able to start forgiving my mother for projecting her pain onto me. I stopped allowing her dark mists of unforgiveness to consume my path.

Forgive Them

When we forgive our parents, it will help us separate their pain from who they really are and what actions they may take. This allows us to filter their words, forgive them more easily and continue our quest.

If one of these choices that your parents made was divorce, it's very important to filter what they say. For example: If one of them is asking you to hate the other or love them more, learn to filter it and let it bounce off you. Just take a step back and have pity on them and think to yourself: *You must still be in so much pain to try and convince me to hate them like you hate them.*

Sometimes, we may just have to forgive our parents for no other reason than the fact that they, too, have to complete their own quest. On their quest, they may be consumed with dark mists. And as a result, they are wandering aimlessly, grasping at anything they can to survive.

Their Life, Their Views

If you have parents that are wandering in their own dark mists, it is very important you don't allow those mists to invade your quest. For example, if your mom divorces your dad and is constantly talking about how she hates men because of one man, do those views have to be your views? No. They don't. That's like saying your mom goes to her favorite restaurant and gets food poisoning. Does that mean you'll never dine out again? The same thing applies. Your mom had one bad experience with one man and, though it may cloud her view of all men in the moment (e.g., swearing she'll never eat out again), make sure you don't let it cloud your view of men forever.

If we allow our parents' negative mists to creep onto our own path, this affects our ability to make wise choices. For example, if your mom finally gets over hating men and marries a wonderful man, but you took on her views of hating men as a child, then what happens when you start dating? Will you like men? It's better to forgive our parents, create our own views of the world and try to keep our skies blue, so that we don't have to undo the negativity of others later.

Love Them No Matter What

We may not always like the choices our parents make—especially if they affect us negatively. But, we can always choose to love them—no matter what. God commanded us to love and honor our parents. Why would He do that if He knew they would mess up and possibly affect our life negatively? Because God knows what they are going through. Only He will judge their actions. If we don't forgive them and love them despite their choices, that may affect us negatively (i.e., patterning your life after theirs—negatively).

Parents are human, and therefore can't be expected to be perfect. As a parent now, I screw up often because of the way I was raised. I hope my children will forgive me my shortcomings and they will do a better job than I am doing with their future kids. Parents are being tempted by Satan as well. Show them kindness, as you would want to be shown if you were going through the same hardships as they are. Our fight is against Satan, not each other. Remember, you chose your parents in the Preexistence for a reason. They are here to either help you or for you to help them or both. Be the warrior of light for them, especially if they are not capable of doing it for you at this time.

Forgiving Yourself

During our quests we will get wounded, have dark mists come over our paths, be tested to the brink, be tempted by Satan and be tried. As a result we will fumble, fall, bleed, doubt, fear, cry and just flat-out fail. We are not perfect. When we fall, we need to pick ourselves up, forgive ourselves and start again.

If we cannot forgive ourselves for the mistakes we've made, then, again, Satan will send dark mists to cloud our views of our potential as heirs in the Kingdom of God.

When we do things that are wrong, guilt is supposed to motivate us to ask for forgiveness. But Satan uses guilt to create shame and hopelessness, to blind us from our individual worth and divine destiny. Don't give in to Satan's promptings of guilt and shame. His plan will always be to put us on a path of darkness. Therefore, use guilt as a motivator to repent, so you can stay true to your course.

Forgiving yourself, as well as others, will bring you freedom from darkness. The freedom that comes from forgiveness will bring the power of choice and healing back into your life. This freedom will also bring peace while climbing mountains, no puppet strings attached to our soul, joy from knowing who we really are and love for the One that created us.

Your Quest for Freedom

Your first quest for freedom begins with writing down the names of all those you feel have harmed you. After you have completed your list, cross out the ones that you have forgiven completely (no bad feelings toward them). Circle the ones that you're not sure if you have forgiven. Put a star beside the ones that you know you haven't forgiven. Then write down how you feel about the ones you haven't forgiven. Decide today if you want them to continue to cloud your view of your divine destiny and fill your life with darkness. Forgive them and remember why you are here, to overcome all obstacles.

Your second quest is to write down any harmful secrets that you may be carrying. If you do have any harmful secrets, write down how they are consuming your life. Write down how much more you fear people now, you doubt yourself, you question people's motives and whether you trust people now. If you are carrying a harmful secret, write down the names of people you feel you can trust and talk to them, get it off your chest and take your power back.

Your third quest is to talk to your parents. Talk to your parents honestly. If they have done anything to hurt you that you may be holding a grudge for, tell them that you want to forgive them for any wrongs they may have done, because you love them. If they are divorced, then tell them to please not badmouth the other, curse the other in front of you, or try to have you hate them.

Your last quest is to dig deep inside and see if there is anything you haven't forgiven yourself for. If there is, then ask yourself why. Do you feel you don't deserve it, or it's too bad, or you don't think you can be forgiven? If there are items you haven't asked for forgiveness for, do so. Ask God to forgive you. As He does, forgive yourself. Then move on.

Once you have moved on from unforgiveness toward yourself and others, you will have just created bluer skies on your quest home to our Heavenly Father.

Forgiveness will set you free.

Prayer will make your stronger.

Love will hold you tighter.

Parents will appreciate your example.

The Quest for Relief

CHAPTER 6

The Quest for Relief
Discover God's plan of justice and mercy

ould it be easier for you to forgive if you saw justice being dealt with promptly? Maybe. Unfortunately, that's not how God works. In the Preexistence, we fought for free agency, the freedom to choose for ourselves whether to make good choices or bad choices. Some will abuse that power. Therefore, because of free agency, this question will always remain the same: Will man do what is right and uplift others or will he do what is wrong and hurt others?

In reality, our free agency is the only thing that we have power over. We can either help others and ourselves when we follow God's plan and do what is right, or we can destroy others and ourselves when we follow Satan's designs and do what is wrong. With this in mind, if God dealt quickly and swiftly with those who did wrong, wouldn't that scare them into doing what is right?

God uses the Spirit of Christ to guide us by gently reminding us what is right and what is wrong. For instance, our Heavenly Father has placed road signs on our path home. But, he cannot force us to follow them. Similarly, God does not allow Satan to force us to be evil. That has to be our choice. But Satan can tempt us to do his will through making poor choices. Everyone has the choice to which path they will choose, and God has two plans that deal with those who choose to abuse their free agency or go down a dark path.

God's Plan of Justice

Though God cannot and will not take away the free agency of man, God can and will use the eternal law of justice. The law of justice demands that someone pay for every sin we commit. Either we pay for our own sins, or Jesus Christ our Savior pays for them. It doesn't matter who, but someone must pay the price. Those who have harmed you or who are harming you will pay for their wrongs in the next life if they do not repent and make amends for their wrongs in this life. If they repent, Christ pays for their sins. If they do not repent, they will pay for their own sins.

Every unrepentant soul will suffer as Christ suffered. Everything that happens on Earth will be made fair in the next life. As stated in Matt 8:12, "But the children of the kingdom shall be cast out into outer darkness: there shall be weeping and gnashing of teeth." Those who follow Satan's plan and harm others will suffer as Christ suffered. In fact, they will suffer until the sin has satisfied the demands of justice. Therefore, let your quest for relief be satisfied through God.

I understand it is hard to see others getting away with their sins here on Earth. But, they will pay the price after they die. God promises this in Luke 18:7, "And shall not God avenge his own elect, which cry day and night unto him, though he bear long with them?" For God is a just God and will not allow sins to go unpunished, unless the sinners have repented. If those who sin do not repent here (which includes making it right with you), they will suffer as Christ suffered. Therefore, there is no need for you to get revenge here on Earth for those who have harmed you. For God's justice will be far more complete than what you could ever inflict upon them.

The Time Needed to Change

Trust God's plan of justice. He knows what He is doing and He will make all things right. In His wisdom, He allows time for those who sin and make mistakes to have a chance to repent and be forgiven. He knows many of us will mess up many times in our life. He knows there will be times we go down the wrong path. He hopes we will repent, make it right with the person we hurt and ultimately learn from our mistakes. God loves us and wants us to learn and grow and use Jesus Christ's atonement to be forgiven.

For example: You have come to a point on your path that you need to cross a great divide. The only way to get across is two sets of rope: one to hold onto and one that you can put your feet on. While crossing this unstable rope, you notice someone on the other side, also crossing. Because the two of you are using the same rope, it makes it very unstable. You find yourself starting to really shake. As a result, the other loses his grip and falls. Would you want God's justice to be handed to you swiftly and promptly or would you want to be given the chance to say you're sorry, try to make amends and learn how not to do it again?

We are all here to learn and grow from our mistakes, and say we're sorry when we have messed up. Being punished immediately would take away our needed time to reflect and change. Hopefully, that is what you'll do. You'll learn from your sins and mistakes and change. If you don't, it will not go well for you on the other side.

Repent here or Pay the price there

If you are one of those who have wronged another person, I implore you to repent. Make amends and change, or you will suffer for everything you've done to others. You may not pay in this life, but you definitely will in the next. Don't be fooled by Satan and think if you got away with it here, you will get away with it there. God will not allow any sin to go unpunished. Either you repent and use Christ's atonement or you will suffer as He did.

Watch out for Satan's Fiery Darts of Lies!

Freedom is doing what I want and getting away with it

It is very important to repent and seek forgiveness here on Earth before you die. Once you are on the other side (spirit world) it is very hard to gain that forgiveness from those who you've harmed and until you do, you will suffer.

To illustrate a deceased person's suffering, let me tell you an experience a friend of mine had. One night, as she was sleeping, a presence woke her up. When she opened her eyes and looked upon him, she instantly knew who it was. It was someone who had harmed her earlier in her life and changed her life forever. She was startled to see him because he had been deceased for quite a while. As she looked upon him, she noticed he was drenched in his tears. She realized those were tears of pain, regret, suffering, and of despair.

He finally spoke and begged her forgiveness for the wrongs he had done to her when he was alive. He told her he would continue to suffer in spirit prison until he was forgiven. She could see he was in a state of sorrow and panic. She felt compassion for him instantly. **Forgiving others and obtaining forgiveness is very real.**

The Innocent

Though God does not demand immediate justice here on Earth, He will take care of justice in the next life. With this in mind, let me explain a truth concerning the innocent. **No matter what has happened to you physically, mentally, emotionally, spiritually, or sexually, your spirit will be and has always been protected.** If you were to die today after someone had raped you, do you think you would carry that insult of abuse to the spirit world when it was forced upon you here? Absolutely not. Physically and emotionally, you might have experienced pain here on Earth. But the abuser cannot touch your spirit.

Your innocence will remain as pure as the day you were born. You are of royal birth and God protects the innocent with His might and healing power. In Luke 4:18 it states, "...he hath sent me to heal the brokenhearted, to preach deliverance to the captives, and recovering of sight to the blind, to set at liberty them that are bruised," He will heal those that are bruised by others.

God's Plan of Mercy

Where there is justice, there has to be mercy. As God's justice claims those who have not repented, so will God's mercy claim the innocent and those that have repented. The innocent who have been harmed by others will have the bands of mercy encircle them and heal their wounds. God will not allow the sinner to go unpunished. So, too, God will not allow the innocent to go unhealed. **Mercy is alive in Christ's atonement.** The innocent can have hope and faith that God will deal justly with those that hurt them. Through God's plan of mercy, the heart of the afflicted will be healed, thus bringing relief to a troubled soul.

God's plan of mercy is so powerful it can pull you out of an eternal Hell and save your life here. For example: let's say while you and a friend are walking along your path you come across a fork in the road. You can choose to either take the path that looks used often, seems faster, but not as safe, or you can take the path less often used, has a longer road, steeper hills, but looks safe. As you're deciding, your friend encourages you to take the road less traveled and safer. Despite your friend's plea to take the safe road, you take the road often traveled because it looks faster. After thirty minutes of walking, you come to a very thin edge along this cliff. Again your friend pleads with you not to go and, though you feel you shouldn't go as well, you do anyway. As you both are side stepping this edge, the edge starts to crumble. You and your friend know you are both about to fall and die so you cry and ask God for help. You tell God you messed up and your friend is not at fault. Because of God's plan of mercy, you are both saved because you repented and your friend was innocent.

Repentance

Those who have harmed others and do not want the demands of justice imposed upon them have the bands of mercy extended to them as well, if they repent. If you come to Jesus Christ and repent with a broken heart and a contrite spirit, you will receive forgiveness through the atonement.

Repentance is three-fold. First you must acknowledge you have done something wrong. Second, you must ask God to forgive you. Third, you must make amends to the one you harmed.

The first two speak for themselves. But the third means you must seek out the one you've harmed, asked for forgiveness, and then try to make it right. For example, I will use the analogy I gave of the tight rope. After you saw the other person fall from the tight rope because of the shaking on your end, you must seek that person, tell him you're sorry and make sure he is okay. If you were to just continue on your way after they fell, you would not gain forgiveness for that mistake—even if you told God you were sorry.

Step three of making amends is very important in obtaining forgiveness. If you do not try to seek the one that you harmed and make it right, then forgiveness from God will not be given to you.

Another important thing to note about repentance is: If you ask God to forgive you on a certain act and then you continue to do that act, you will not obtain forgiveness. For example, let's say you are bullying others at school and you hurt someone deeply so you decide to seek forgiveness. Then, a couple of weeks later, you bully someone again. Both of those sins would be on your head. Repentance starts with asking for forgiveness from God and those whom you've harmed. Forgiveness is extended when God knows we are truly sorry and we do not repeat the act.

Some things are harder to be forgiven of than others. For example, if you had beaten someone up and badly hurt them, this would be harder, and take longer, to be forgiven for than if you were to yell at a brother or sister. Though some sins are harder to be forgiven than others, it's important you seek forgiveness in all things, so that you may get back on your path for this quest and not have to pay the price in the next life.

Having an unrepentant soul will darken your path more than any sin or mistake. If you do not seek forgiveness for your sins, then the Spirit of the Lord will withdraw and Satan will have His turn at you.

Repenting and trying to make good decisions will give you the breastplate of righteousness. The breastplate of righteousness does not symbolize being perfect, it symbolizes trying to do your best through righteous living (i.e., deeds, acts, repentance). This breastplate guards against the temptations and fiery darts of Satan. Without this protection, you are an easy target for Satan.

2 Pet. 1:1, "obtained like... faith with us through the righteousness of God."

Beware of the lies Satan tells

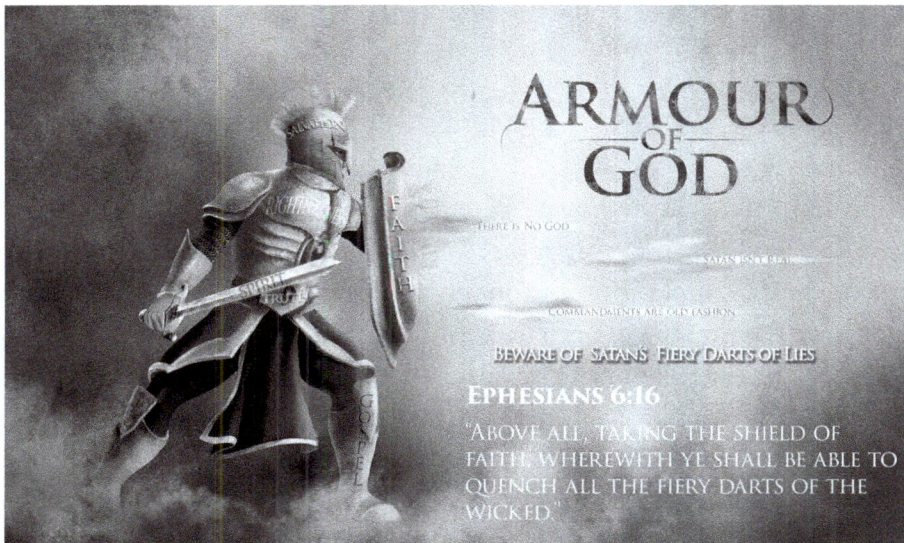

ARMOUR OF GOD

BEWARE OF SATANS FIERY DARTS OF LIES

EPHESIANS 6:16

"ABOVE ALL, TAKING THE SHIELD OF FAITH, WHEREWITH YE SHALL BE ABLE TO QUENCH ALL THE FIERY DARTS OF THE WICKED."

Just Because You Can doesn't Mean You Should

With the increasing amount of darkness in our world, there comes a concept from Satan that many of the youth are accepting. The concept is: Just because you can do something to others, gives you the permission you should. Let me give you some examples of *just because you can doesn't mean you should*. Just because you're bigger than someone else, doesn't mean you should pick on them. Just because you are being bullied at home, doesn't mean you should bully others at school. Just because your friends are doing something bad, doesn't mean you should. Just because you can have sex with anyone because you're good looking, doesn't mean you should.

Satan will try to convince us that, because we can do something, we should do something and that's where freedom lies. Satan is a liar, for those we have harmed we will have justice served on our head, here or in the next life. Be careful what you do in this life, for there is always a ripple effect when it comes to our choices.

The Ripple Effect

God has given us the power to choose. As a result, we may feel *just because we can do* in our lives *we should*. Watch out. Satan does not tell you about the ripple effect of your choices. What you do to cause others harm will be accounted unto you until it stops (the ripple effect). Let me give you an example of the harmful effect of abusing your free agency and hurting others.

Let's say you come from an abusive home where your father constantly hits you. You feel, because you have been hurt, you should be able to hurt others. One day, you feel especially angry because your father hit you before you left home for school. As you're on your way to school, you see this smaller kid (let's call him Bobby) coming down your side of the street. As he gets close enough to you to walk by, he accidentally bumps into you. As a result, you lose it. You feel, in that moment, that you have the right to hurt Bobby. You're pissed off at the world and you've been hurt by your father.

With the anger built up inside of you, you hurt Bobby really badly. Once you are done, you go your own way, leaving Bobby there groaning in pain. After an hour lying there on the sidewalk, Bobby finally gets up to go home. His home is already full of pain and suffering. Bobby has nothing at home to comfort him. All he has at home is a mom dying of cancer. He is left alone to now deal with not only taking care of his mom, but of being beaten up and having no one to talk to about it. Bobby's anger builds. He feels life is serving him up a lump of coal. He, too, lashes out at the next person he sees.

The kid (Tom) Bobby hurts because of his anger, now, in turn, hurts someone else (Joe) and so on. According to the ripple effect, the demand of justice will be served to not just Bobby, who did the damage on Tom, but to the person who started it. Our choices are so powerful that they can affect generations for good and bad (the ripple effect).

The same thing applies to a good deed. If you see a boy drop his books in front of his locker and you walk over to help him, this, in turn, makes him feel awesome. Then he assists another person who also was having a bad day. All of those good deeds that day will be accounted unto you for good, because you started the ripple effect of uplifting others.

Choose wisely. Your choices could affect hundreds of people for good or bad. With that said, if you are the one hurt, please do not pass it down the line. You never know what circumstances the afflicter came from. Forgive the one who hurt you and stop the ripple effect. Not only will this help you here, but it will help the afflicter in the next life (which will help you).

If you are the one who started a negative ripple effect in your life and in the lives of others with your poor choices, I recommend you seek forgiveness through the atonement and try to make amends. Making amends by doing a good deed for those who you have hurt can reverse the negative effects into positive ones. You can't take back what you did (that's what the atonement is for), but you can try and make it right through helping others.

Don't Judge too quickly

You never know what circumstances others may be going through. For instance, I have found that many bullies come from abusive homes. They are angry and have not forgiven those who harmed them. They feel justified in harming others.

My daughter proved this point in third grade. A bully in her school, whom we'll call Lisa, constantly pushed her and other kids down, butted in line, called others names and tried to create fights. One day, my daughter tried my lesson in kindness with Lisa. After about a week of my daughter inviting Lisa to eat with her, play with her and do homework with her, Lisa's heart was changed. They became friends. Later, my daughter discovered that Lisa's parents had just gotten a divorce. Lisa was very angry about it.

Sometimes, all bullies need is someone to be kind to them, listen to them, love them, uplift them and befriend them. Don't be too quick to judge another. Each of us is on our individual quests. Each has to conquer Satan. Each will have trials to overcome. And each will be searching for relief, help them find it with kindness.

My Quest for Relief

As I was growing up, I saw a lot of pain and suffering in my home because of my parents' divorce. I saw my mom struggling to raise eight kids by herself. The other four were either in college or on missions for our church. My mother used to badmouth my father all the time and make us feel guilty when we went with him. She pushed her kids to be perfect in everything we did, especially cleanliness. She verbally and mentally abused us when things weren't going her way, all because she was emotionally blind from the divorce.

For years, I didn't understand why my mom treated us so badly and felt so out of control. For Heaven sakes, we had just lost our father in the divorce. But as time went on, and after running away from home and living with my father, I started to understand. I found out my own mother did not have the best upbringing. She had been rejected in a lot of ways by her family. So, when my father rejected her by getting a divorce, it absolutely crushed her. Furthermore, I learned that when people feel out of control with their feelings and their own life, they will try to control everything and everyone around them, believing it will fill that void.

When I finally understood that my mom's worst fear was to be rejected and she was spinning out of control, my eyes were open to why she couldn't see what she was doing to her children. I learned then never to judge anyone until you walk in their shoes. As I understood her grief, it became easier to forgive her for her misdeeds. And as I did, I found relief from my negative feelings.

Everyone has a quest that is full of trials and challenges that they must go through and no one will do it perfectly. After my parents' divorce, my mom was just barely surviving. She could barely save her children from the pain they were going through. I found the relief I was searching for by understanding why my mom did certain things. Relief will come when we don't judge others, but try to understand what they're going through and forgive them.

Christ's New Law

Could you imagine what the world would be like if everyone took into consideration what others may be going through? Better yet, what would happen if everyone realized this Earthly life was a test and our enemy is not each other, but Satan? To get there, we must start with the golden rules: *Do unto others as you would have done to you. Judge another as you would like to be judged.* If you want our Heavenly Father to be merciful to you for your transgressions, you must forgive others who sin against you.

For example: Let's say you're on your path home, when you come across someone who's hurt. You think to yourself, *if I stop now I will lose a couple of hours.* So, you start to walk off. Then, something inside you tells you to help him. So you turn back, bandage his wounds and help him on his way. When you get back on your path, you feel pretty good inside.

A day later, while still trekking on your path, you come across treacherous terrain that goes straight up. As you are climbing you start to slip. You scream for help. Just before you lose your last grip, someone grabs your hand and pulls you up. Once you are on safe ground, you look at the stranger to thank him. To your surprise, it is the man you helped the day before.

Our Heavenly Father asks us to treat others as we would want to be treated. We are not living in the time of Moses, where an eye for an eye was the rule. We are living in a time that desperately needs love, kindness and forgiveness. When Jesus Christ brought the new laws:

- *Turn the other cheek;*
- *Treat others as you'd want to be treated;*
- *Love your enemies;*
- *Pray for those who despitefully use you;*

He did so with us in mind. Jesus knew the world would, eventually, become full of pain and suffering. He knew the only way to keep us from being swallowed up in it, is to grasp onto God's laws of kindness, trust, love and healing. God knew an eye for an eye will never bring peace like love and forgiveness can in a world that needs it so badly.

We must always strive to do the right thing—no matter what is returned—and hope that God will account it for our good. As we allow God's justice to claim those who have hurt us, seek repentance when we have messed up, be careful of the choices we make that affect others, and treat others as we would want to be treated, we will find relief from the sorrows in this life. Relief comes when we do our part in forgiving and we let God do his part in judging.

TRUTH

Eph. 6:14, "Stand therefore, having your loins girt about with truth..."

As you use the belt of truth, the truth that God will deal justly with those that have harmed us, you will be set free. We are on this quest and our choices of forgiving, loving, and accepting will always be rewarded, whether other humans return in kind. Therefore, be true to yourself, others, and our Heavenly Father by causing positive ripple effects in your life. As you are true to your course back home, you will find ultimate relief when hardships come.

Your Quest for Relief

Your first quest for relief is to search within. See if there are any grudges, feelings of revenge, or hopes of someone else getting hurt. If you find you have not forgiven another because justice hasn't been served to them here on Earth, seek God's forgiveness. Repent for your continued ill-feelings toward that person who hurt you and ask God to do His will on them.

The second quest for relief is to repent for those things *you* have done that have harmed others or yourself. After you have sought God's forgiveness, go to the person and ask for forgiveness. Try to make it right. You may be surprised that this course of action brings you a new friend instead of an enemy.

Your third quest is to see if you are doing anything that is contrary to the new law of Christ. Are you doing things in your life that will bring dishonor to your name? See what kind of ripple effects you are creating by your choices. If they are negative ripple effects, repent and start creating positive ones. In fact, I challenge you to do ten good deeds in one day and see what the Heavens return in kind. Then write down what happens.

And finally, I want you to treat others as you would want to be treated for a week and see what that does for your self-esteem, your relationship with God, your love for others and your overall confidence.

Your job is to forgive. God's job is to judge.

Treat others as you would WANT to be treated.

Create such positive ripple effects that
your future children will feel it.

The Quest for Self-Control

CHAPTER 7

The Quest for Self Control
Discover Satan's plan of deception

As we continue on this quest, there will be times when we will be tempted by things that are not good for us. Satan will do whatever he can to slow us down, steer us off course, darken our views, be our puppeteer, weaken our souls and poison our bodies. He will try to deprive us of our eternal reward. His biggest target is our body.

During your quest, and because of many hard obstacles you've encountered, you may find yourself starving for affection, for love, for compassion, for acceptance, for relief and for peace. When people are starving, they typically will eat anything. But be careful what you put into your body. Your choice could mean the difference between Satan controlling you and you controlling you.

Watch out for Satan's fiery Darts of Lies!

Poison won't harm you

Don't Let a Caramel Apple Fool You

As you're on your quest, you start to feel hungry. As you do, you notice these caramel apples within your reach. When you look at them, the only thing you can see is this beautiful outer shell of caramel that covers the entire apple. It looks sweet and gooey. Your glands start to salivate, and you think: *Boy I can't wait to eat this delicious caramel apple; it will fill my soul, for I am starving.*

Upon the first bite, a disgusting flavor fills your mouth and you find that the apple inside is rotten and poisonous. You feel betrayed. How could the outer part of the apple that is covered with this caramel look so good and enticing, while hiding its true nature of it being poisonous inside? And, how is it that these appeared along my path as soon as I felt I was hungry?

Satan is smart, he will tempt you when your need is evident. When he knows your starving, he's going to make what he is offering to look as tempting and enticing as possible. Therefore, be careful what you put into your body. The side effects can be deadly as poison.

Poison

Why would I use the word *poison* to describe the inside of this caramel apple? Because there are different types of poison. Some poisons are fast-acting and deadly. Others are slow and unnoticed. The same concept applies to sins. Some sins are more traumatic to the soul immediately, while other sins take a little bit longer to show their damage. But ultimately, the poison of sin will wreck havoc in your life. Satan will make sin look appealing so it can be tempting to us. Do you think Satan would tempt you with something that you knew would kill you immediately, or try and tempt you with a rotten apple?

Remember, Satan is the most cunning, deceptive, hateful, evil spirit that ever existed. He will do everything he can to cloud your view of what he is tempting you with. Satan does not, and will not, put the poison symbol on things you're about to take because he knows you wouldn't take it. Instead, he covers sin with a beautiful outer shell like caramel, so that he may hide the true nature of the poisonous apple inside.

Watch out for Satan's fiery Darts of Lies!

Fun is our ultimate Goal

One method Satan uses is the media as a source to convince us that it doesn't matter what we put into our bodies. Fun is our ultimate goal. What Satan doesn't show us through the media is the results of partaking of the poison. Why would He? His main goal is to try to convince us that drugs, porn, alcohol, premarital sex and smoking are the only way to live.

If Satan can't convince you to partake of the whole poisonous caramel apple, he will make you believe that biting just a little bit into it won't do very much damage. He will try to convince you that, because you are starving, you have every right to quench your starvation no matter the method. Beware. No matter how starving you are, don't be fooled into eating Satan's caramel apple. Your starvation will not be quenched. In fact, Satan's enticement will only leave you more famished.

The caramel may look wonderful and tasty. It may even look perfect. But watch out for the poison inside the apple, for it will quickly or slowly destroy who you are. Satan knows who we are, so he has created sins to be in opposition to God's commandments. He knows when we disobey God's commands, it is another way he can get us off course and weaken us. If he succeeds, then we are allowing him to be our puppet master.

Before we left, our Heavenly Father gave us the armor of God to defend against Satan. The one that protects our bodies the most is the breastplate of righteousness. The breastplate of righteousness encourages us to keep our minds and bodies clean from filth and darkness. As a breastplate protects our body from any arrow, sword, or any other weapon aimed at destroying our most vital parts, similarly, our Heavenly Father wants us to use the breastplate of righteousness to quench the fiery darts of Satan's temptation, deception and poisonous lies. Our Heavenly Father wants us to be happy. And true happiness comes from keeping our minds and bodies clean, and, ultimately, conquering our quest.

Starvation

Most people will be tempted to eat caramel apples along their path because they are starving. Through starvation, Satan will try to convince us that his offerings can dull our pain. Satan is a liar. None of his methods will ever solve any problem that we are faced with. The only thing that will solve our problems is to forgive those who have harmed us, ask God to heal us and then to learn from it. In other words starvation is only quenched with real foods (tree of life).

When Starvation Begins

There may be times that you are in so much pain because of what you've gone through, that you may be convinced that eating the caramel apple will somehow dull the pain or poison the other person who harmed you. It won't. If you choose to partake of the caramel apple then it will poison your own soul, which will make the pain even worse. For instance, if you were to get bit by a rattlesnake, would anyone feel the

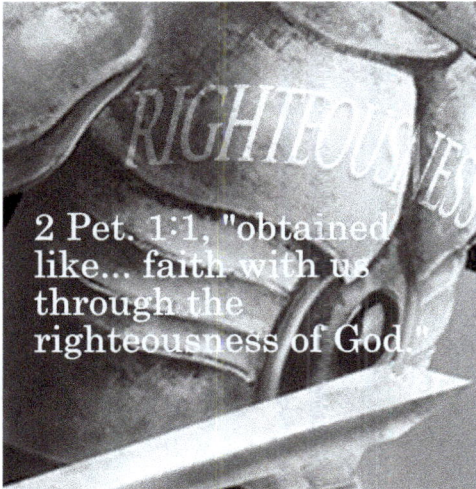

2 Pet. 1:1, "obtained like... faith with us through the righteousness of God."

pain or get the poison? No, just you. Trying to dull the pain because of harmful acts done to us through Satan's methods will *never* be in your best interest. And thinking you are making others suffer through you poisoning yourself is not reality.

Satan tempts us with many "caramel apples." Each has its own consequences and degrees of darkness. Each will thwart our efforts of overcoming our trials, forgiving those who have harmed us, seeking out for God's help, feeling the Spirit, using the Savior's atonement and, ultimately, returning back to our Heavenly Father victorious.

Starving for Love

Satan's Way - As you're walking along your path, you might feel lonely (parents divorced) and unloved. One day you notice some people on a darker path having sex, so you watch. As you watch, Satan convinces you to partake of the poisonous caramel apple of pornography by watching others as well. He convinces you that if you can see others "having sex" that it will quench your hunger for love. What Satan did not tell you, as you look at porn, is that this love is not real, but created by him. He also did not tell you that, as you look at porn, you'll find yourself becoming more controlling, depressed, narcissistic, anxious and have a low self-concept. Such results create you not loving yourself now.

If you continue to partake of this type of caramel apple to quench your hunger for love, Satan will cloud your view of what God created woman and man to be. He will cloud your view that our Heavenly Father created women to be viewed as loving, kind, nurturing, mothering, and held in high regard. The poison in this apple will make you blind to the true nature of women and men. As a result, you'll view women as a means to fulfill pleasures. You will see love as self-serving and not self-giving. Sex will become the tool for pleasure and not the tool to bring a man and a woman together.

The more you eat of this caramel apple of porn, the more women become objects and relationships become boring. You will find that the poison inside your system from porn will cause you to view any love as fake, animalistic, a means to an end and ultimately a self-serving tool. God's love will soon not seem as important to you once you are consumed with Satan's type of love "Porn." The poison in this caramel apple will darken your view of love and relationships, especially when real love finally appears. The poison of pornography will slowly kill your soul. As a result, your quest will become boring, lonely and full of self-loathing.

God's Way - Love comes from reaching out to those that care about us and being vulnerable. When we communicate our need for love to our parents and God, love will come in a pure form. As you feel real love from others, your love for yourself will too increase. And when the time is right, true love will be recognized (future spouse).

Starving for Affection

As you partake of the caramel apple of pornography and your views of women and men are being tainted, Satan will then convince you to partake of the second type of poisonous caramel apple: premarital sex. Your starvation for affection becomes even greater after you have tried to quench your starvation for love. But remember, how you tried to quench your starvation for love was not God's way, but Satan's way. Similarly, how we try and quench our thirst for affection will determine whether it is quenched.

God created sex to be between a man and a woman who have saved themselves for the honeymoon night. True love and fulfilling affection through the act of sex comes only when you have completely given yourself to another. And that type of commitment can only be achieved through marriage. This commandment is found in Duet 5:18, "Neither shalt thou commit adultery." Committing adultery is not just having sex with another married individual, but having sex before you're married.

The poison of having sex before marriage is of course STDs, getting pregnant out of wedlock and ultimately feeling empty inside. The first two are widely known, but the one that Satan tries to hide from you is the one that can leave you emotionally scarred, feeling empty inside and eventually leaving a huge void in your life.

Sex is not only an avenue to have children in marriage, but also to bond two souls into one. When you give yourself to another person through the act of sex, you are actually giving them a part of you (emotionally, mentally, physically, and spiritually). Therefore, when you have sex with multiple people you are giving them a piece of yourself that you can't get back. As a result, after each act of intercourse, your soul believes it is becoming one with the other person, but because there is no lasting commitment, like in marriage, it emotionally tears you apart. Until eventually you become emotionally scarred and callous. You will come to find that when you do finally find the one you want to be with for the rest your life, it will be very difficult to really bond to that one person because you have casually given yourself to many.

Have you noticed that those who partake in casual sex are more likely to get into drugs, alcohol, porn and gangs than those that don't? Having sex outside of marriage will create a void inside of you, which you will try to fill through these other means. The safest and most rewarding sex you will ever have is inside of marriage. God created it to be that way. Waiting adds value to a marriage and to your self-worth. It makes the marriage special and worth fighting for in times of trouble.

Please note: Sex is not bad, just like driving a car is not bad. But you must wait until you have a driver's license to drive, as you must wait to have a marriage license to have sex. God is the one who created sex. All He asks is for us is to wait until we have our marriage license. Then, we are free to enjoy sex to its fullest and bond two souls together as one.

Satan will try to convince you that love is love and affection is affection, no matter the form. Satan always takes a truth and twists it into a lie. True love and real affection comes from the sweet reward of marrying your best friend. If sex is placed on hold until you take your vows what could you truly discover about the other person? How deep could the relationship go? When your relationship is deep, sex becomes the icing on the cake. If sex is the icing and the relationship is the cake, how much weight does the cake hold in times of trouble? Everything, it is the cake that holds the icing together not the other way around.

As you continue on your quest, there may be times when you are starved for affection. There may be times when others come on your path and convince you to have sex. Don't be fooled. Those that are looking to fulfill their own needs will not stick around when times get rough. God's plan is for us to go on our own individual quests at the beginning and then be joined by another through marriage. If two are working towards the same goal, what are your chances of conquering your quests? Strong. So take care to not give your most prized possession (virginity) to another, for the poison of premarital sex can blind your eyes when your true love is finally right in front of your face.

Starving for Relief

Satan's Way - I want you to picture yourself back on your path. Now at the moment you feel weak inside because you've been harmed by another (i.e., molested, bullied). You don't want to feel the pain anymore of reliving it over and over again in your mind and you choose not to forgive, so you partake of the poisonous caramel apple of drugs. Upon the first bite you feel a little dizzy. You may think: *Nothing to worry about.* As you continue to eat that caramel apple of drugs you start to feel your senses and stability becoming wishy-washy. After feeling these bad side effects, you put the apple down and think that is the worst of it.

As you continue to walk along your path you find your path becoming very dark and filled with crevasses. As you decide whether you will cross or not, you find yourself not being able to think clearly and Satan convinces you to cross anyway. As you do, you fall because your mind was altered and you couldn't see straight. Do you think Satan will go down and pick you up and make sure you're okay? No. He is going to laugh that He convinced you to partake of the caramel apple of drugs, fall off the cliff and allow Him to be your puppeteer.

Drugs alter our minds and darken our paths and make it very difficult to conquer our quest when Satan's strings are attached. They can give us the illusion that everything is great—until we fall (i.e., become addicted, brain dead). As a result, your starvation for relief only got worse. Satan will never help you find relief. The poison in drugs can be quick and deadly, or slow and painful.

God's Way - Relief comes from forgiving those that have harmed us, seeking help from others, communicating our frustrations to those that can help (parents), and letting God's justice claim the afflicter. Relief comes from not letting what has happened to us define our next choices, but healing from it with God's help, so that we can release the pain.

Starving for Acceptance

Satan's Way - With the rise in divorce, single-parent homes, teenage pregnancies, and other less-than-ideal home lives, we may be looking for acceptance in any form. Our Heavenly Father knows everyone wants someone to help them conquer their quests, defeat the dragon, point the right direction and accept them for who they are. But don't be fooled through the poisonous caramel apple of gangs or other groups that do not have your best interest at heart.

For example, let's say you find yourself on your path and everyone you thought should help you on your quest has abandoned you. As Satan watches you feel discouraged and lonely, He places another on your path. Upon first glance at this other person, you feel you shouldn't join him. But through constant temptation and peer pressure, you join the group.

As you go along with this group, you find that they murder, rape and pillage every village they go through. Did you find the acceptance you are looking for or did you find more trouble, pain and hurt than you were in before? Satan always makes sin, or groups, look tempting and sweet. Once you partake of this poisonous apple, it's hard to walk away without the poison still in your system or following you. **If you join a gang just to feel accepted, what are your chances of coming out of it alive?** The poison of gangs is both a deadly poison to you and your loved ones.

God's Way - Real acceptance for who you are inside comes from within. If you are okay with who you are and what you're made of (a Child of God) the other kind of acceptance will not be so sought out. As you accept yourself as a child of a King, then others will be drawn to you. You will find that the "group" you created by knowing you are special will help uplift others, which in turn will make you feel even more accepted.

Starving for Peace

Satan's Way - So far on your quest, you've already come across the dragon, trials, temptations, and others trying to either wound you, or knock you off your treacherous terrain. Thus, you are starving for some peace. Satan tempts you to partake of the poisonous caramel apple of alcohol to quench that starvation for peace. He will convince you that alcohol brings peace to any troubled soul. He will have you believe it can dull your pain and make your problems go away.

What Satan doesn't tell you is that the dull feeling that comes from drinking alcohol also greatly alters your senses, enhances your negative emotions, invites Satan in and inhibits your common sense. So here you are walking along your path and drinking every chance you can because of the many things that have happened to you. One day, you drink too much and pass out. Someone takes advantage of you (date rape). You're angry, even more now, so you continue to drink a lot. Each drink slowly makes things worse. The next day while walking along your path, you fumble and fall off (you drink and drive and end up killing someone).

Now, the consequence that comes from killing someone makes it very difficult for you to get back on the path that will bring you peace. You can't find peace through alcohol consumption. Peace comes only from dealing with the problem face on, not trying to drown them. Beware. When you are impaired, you could harm yourself and others. The poison in alcohol is poison to you and those around you.

God's Way - True peace comes from forgiving those that have harmed us and asking God to heal us. Only true peace will heal our pain, sharpen our senses and positively change our emotions. Peace comes from knowing we have conquered and overcome our trials successfully. Peace also comes from staying true to ourselves, despite what happens to us.

There will be many poisonous caramel apples in your life tempting you to take a bite. They all have their Earthly consequences, and potentially eternal consequences. But there is one poisonous caramel apple that has an irreversible effect on you and all those in your life—and that is suicide.

Starvation for Compassion

Because of the hurt that we will feel by others abusing their free agency (i.e., being raped, molested, bullied, beaten, or harmed in any other way) we may be starving for compassion. Compassion is wishing that someone will listen, counsel, and console us. Recently this has become Satan's most tempting poisonous caramel apple along people's path. Satan will make you believe that if you kill yourself it will be better on the other side. Don't be fooled. Suicide will stop your quest dead in its tracks (literally.)

Remember in the Preexistence we made promises to others in our family, our Heavenly Father, and ourselves to conquer our quest, fight the dragon and come out victorious. If you commit suicide, you are not only breaking the promises you made, but you are giving up on your quest to become an heir in the Kingdom of God. That opportunity is given ONCE. Furthermore it will cause more pain and suffering to your loved ones. Please seek help if you are having suicidal thoughts. Suicide is not the answer. The poison in suicide is deadly here and in the afterlife.

Finding compassion starts with talking about our needs and wants with loved ones. Think about it, what is the first thing Satan convinces when considering suicide? That no one cares or understands your pain, right? If you don't talk about your pain then, of course they can't show compassion or try and understand what you're going through. Finding compassion starts with you reaching out to others.

My Quest for Compassion

When I was twelve years old, my mom moved me down to California to train to be a professional tennis player. After a year of my living with two different families, my mom decided to rent out her house in Utah and she and my little sister moved down to California. She felt I had so much potential to become a professional tennis player that she needed to push me hard.

When she moved down, I was a freshman in a brand-new high school once again. I had no friends and no one to talk to and all I did was play tennis. My mom's drive for me to be a professional tennis player clouded her view that I was still her daughter and still a kid. Every time I lost, she would yell at me and push me to do better. During the fights, she would remind me that she moved down to California, rented out her house, and uprooted her family, all so I could pursue the chance to become a professional tennis player.

This pattern of screaming took place three or four times a week. The guilt I felt was immense, not just because I didn't want to play anymore and my mom had moved out there for me, but because my little sister was miserable being there without any friends either. To top it off and add to the anger of my mom, my dad only lived thirty miles away and she knew I wanted to see him more.

I felt stuck and hopeless. I had no one to talk to and felt no compassion from my mom. As I continued to lose, the screaming got worse. After about six months of this hell, the only thing that started looking good to me was to commit suicide. But whenever I started to think about it, I had second thoughts.

Then one night my mom and I got into a huge fight. She grabbed a knife and jabbed it at my stomach, only breaking the skin. She knew she had gone too far this time. I ran out of the apartment at ten o'clock at night, determined never to come back. I remember thinking that this life was too hard and I thought of all the reasons why I'd be better off leaving this world.

As I was walking to this park that we lived by, I was totally oblivious as to how unsafe it was to be walking by myself at age thirteen late at night. The area we were in was known for its crime. I noticed a man sitting in the park watching me. I found it curious, but my anger blinded me to the fact that he could possibly hurt me. I sat down and started to pray. I told the Heavenly Father every reason why I wanted to die and then I asked him for one reason why I should keep living.

No answer came immediately, so I got up to start walking around. As I was walking around the park, I finally noticed this man staring at me. I was now conscious of the fact that I was in a dangerous position, so I started to walk towards home. The man started to follow me, so I walked faster. When I looked back to see where he was I saw his face look as white as a ghost. Suddenly, he ran as fast as he could to get away from me.

The feeling came over me that I had a guardian angel protect me and this man saw him. I realized that my quest was not over. I felt in that moment that if my Heavenly Father had a guardian angel watching over me, then He must want me to still live. I ran back home, jumped into bed and thanked Him for His protection. Our Heavenly Father showed me compassion that day when I needed it most. He can do the same for you, but you must ask.

Finding Filling Food for our Souls

Our Heavenly Father loves us very much. He knows we will be hungry for affection when affection is deprived, need love when love is withheld, peace when peace is the last thing we feel, acceptance when we feel all alone and want relief when we are drowning in despair. Therefore, our Heavenly Father has provided the means to fill our souls when they are hungry.

This Heavenly food (tree of life) is in the form of the Gospel of Jesus Christ, forgiveness, deep relationships, families, parents, friends, the atonement, and all other good gifts He has placed on our path. For some of you, deep relationships, stable families, honorable parents, and good friends may be missing on your path. But the Gospel of Jesus Christ, forgiveness and the atonement are always readably available.

GOSPEL

Eph. 6.15, "And your feet shod with the preparation of the gospel of peace;"

Through faith, repentance, and baptism in His church, and through the Spirit, we can find peace, love, joy, deep relationships, and indispensable shoes. The shoes of the Gospel can quench our hunger and keep us from going down dark paths. Therefore don't

be fooled by Satan's tempting, poisonous caramel apples. They will do more harm than you could imagine. They have the potential of stopping your progress, giving you harder challenges on your quest, making you feel weaker and more confused about your direction and, ultimately, keeping you unprotected from the dragon and His puppet strings. The shoes of the Gospel can always keep us one step ahead of Satan and walking clear of His poisonous caramel apples.

Part of our quest here on Earth is to gain self-control, though many are giving in by partaking of every caramel apple they see. Many do this, because they don't realize they are on a quest to return to our Heavenly Father as heirs in His Kingdom. As part of your first quest in chapter one, you came to know that you are on a quest designed by our Heavenly Father to be tested, tried, and challenged in order to prove yourself worthy to be an heir in His Kingdom. I hope that bringing to your awareness Satan's designs and plans of placing as many caramel apples as He can in your path, that you will make better decisions. Remember Satan does not have a body. Therefore, He will do anything He can to help you destroy yours.

The great news of Christ's Gospel and the atonement is if you have been tempted because of your challenges and hardships to partake of any of Satan's poisonous caramel apples, you can be forgiven. When you repent of the things you've done wrong, you are given the antidote for the poison you have inside your system. As long as you are alive, it's never too late. It's just a choice. You have the choice to choose today to start fresh, make better choices, have your poor choices cured, get back on your path and defeat Satan.

Your Quest for Self-Control

Start your quest for self-control by writing down the voids or hungers you have in your life. Then write down the wants and needs that you feel will satisfy this hunger.

Second quest is, find other ways (i.e., faith, the Gospel, forgiveness, good friends, deep relationships...) that can quench your hunger. By finding other ways of coping with the voids we feel in our life, we will be in more control of our life.

Post on your wall what alternatives you have for your hunger (i.e. starvation for acceptance, join a sports team...)

Your third quest for self-control is to write down the poisonous caramel apples you are currently partaking of. Once you have acknowledged the caramel apples in your life and have realized that Satan is just trying to send you down a dark path, write down the ways you can overcome these temptations and cut the strings He has attached to your soul. If you find some hard to overcome seek help, especially from God. I promise you will feel better about life and yourself with a clean body and your senses intact.

Your final quest is, write down what you will do today and the rest of your life in order to avoid the caramel apples in your path, so that you can conquer this quest faithfully and honorably as heirs in God's Kingdom. You are stronger than Satan; prove it to him by kicking those caramel apples off your path completely.

Caramel Apples are there to tempt us.

Heavenly food is there to feed us.

Self-control is there to strengthen us.

Strength will help us defeat the dragon.

The Quest for Hope

CHAPTER 8

The Quest for Hope
Discover your real support system

O ur quest for hope begins when we realize that we need help along our path. Hope occurs when we have faith that things in our life will come to pass. Having faith is hoping for things not seen, but true. For instance, let's say you have partaken of some poisonous apples in your life. You must have faith that, through repentance, Christ's atonement will forgive you and heal you, and hope that God will use those experiences to your benefit.

Hope is the power behind our drive to live, change, endure and complete our quest, despite the fact we have been bruised, wounded, poisoned, challenged and tried. Change is the biggest part hope plays in our life. During our quest, all of us will mess up. If we do not have hope that we can change and be forgiven then why try?

Hope is what helps us forgive, live and trust again when we have been harmed, bruised and beaten. Sometimes, when all seems lost, all we can do is have hope for a better future, hope that we will be healed, hope that our life will turn out okay and hope that will be blessed for our good deeds. Without hope, we would live in darkness. Through Christ's atonement, our Heavenly Father brought hope as a light in the darkness, peace in the despair, strength to the weary, healing to the sick and faith during the unknown.

Without hope in our lives, during many of our trials, we would be lost, unforgiving, hateful and unwilling to change. Hope is what helps us be unselfish, kind, loving, generous and compassionate. Hope is what Satan is fighting to take away from us. If we do not have hope that our deeds would be rewarded or that change is possible, then we would live a life based on selfish desires, evil acts and riotous living. Having faith that the atonement will wipe our sins clean and hope that Christ's mercy will make up the difference will help us conquer our quest with honor.

An Earthly Guardian Angel

Hope is essential when we have so many trials and obstacles along our path. Help from one another can help us keep our hopes up when those obstacles become extremely hard. Therefore, everyone should have someone who believes in them, and supports and encourages them to make good decisions. Someone that will be there for you when you're struggling with what direction you should choose, when warding off Satan's temptations and when you are feeling down. This someone I will call an Earthly Guardian Angel.

An Earthly Guardian Angel is someone who will help you change, figure the things out when you've messed up and be there to help you battle the dragon. Everyone on Earth should have at least one person who will help them succeed on their quest.

Our Heavenly Father never intended us to make this quest alone. Even though it is up to us to make good choices, our Heavenly Father has placed family, friends and others in our lives to help us when we are confused about what choices to make. We all need someone to help keep our hopes up when we are feeling down and discouraged.

When we are trying to change and do what is right, Satan will become even more persistent in trying to have us mess up again. But when you have two people fighting against the dragon, your chances of success have doubled. Therefore, it is very important to find someone here on Earth that you can counsel with, listen to and bounce ideas off. If our Heavenly Father wanted us to complete this quest alone, then each one of us would've been born on our own island.

Everyone needs someone who can give them feedback and be honest with them. An Earthly Guardian Angel is someone to be a check and balance for you to make sure your ideas aren't crazy and could hurt someone else when you feel your anger is over flowing.

A perfect example is the recent shootings at the movie theater on July 20, 2012 in Aurora, Colorado, during a midnight screening of the film *The Dark Knight Rises*. In this example the shooter was a loner, silent and angry. Either he did not tell others his intentions and share his feelings, or he was not being heard. How might things have been different if he had an Earthly Guardian Angel in his life?

My Quest for Hope

During my sophomore year in high school, I lived in California with my dad. I found myself needing support desperately because my mom was so upset that I had ran away. She did anything she could to get me back, including, contacting my tennis coach, the principal of my school and people in my church to tell them what a horrible mistake I'd made. She told them that my father was brainwashing me and that I was a victim and needed counsel from someone.

She would write me letters every week telling me how I had wrecked her life, that I was the devil's daughter, that she was going to kill herself, that I had abandoned my little sister and how much she needed me. The guilt was destroying me. I was actually considering going back and living with her again. It would have been the worst mistake of my life.

I was very confused and depressed and when I went to my father for advice, he would tell me she was crazy and not to worry about it. Unfortunately, I was the type of kid that did worry about it. I couldn't stand hurting someone else's feelings. I didn't have any friends talk to and, although my dad was trying to help me, he was biased. He couldn't stand her. The thing that took its toll on me the most was her telling me that she was going to kill herself. I realized I couldn't overcome this by myself. So, I asked God to help me and to send me someone that could help me get through this, for I felt I was drowning.

Our Heavenly Father sent me an Earthly Guardian Angel. She was a leader in the young women's group in my church; her name was Cindy. Cindy noticed I was struggling and that I was feeling very down and depressed. She helped me believe I was in the right place and that I had made a good decision to leave my mom, especially after the stories I told her about what my mom had done and was doing to me. She explained that now that I was in a healthy environment, I could start healing from all the hell I had gone through.

There were times when I would start to doubt again, but I knew I could call and drop by and talk with Cindy. On those bad days of doubt, we would talk for hours. She would put her arm around me and let me know everything would be okay. I believe that without Cindy helping me and encouraging me, I would have drowned in my despair and confusion.

Drowning

There will be times along your quest that you will feel that all is lost. At times like these, it is important to find someone who believes in you, listens to, counsels you and helps you with your trials and challenges.

For example: While on your quest you come across a small lake. Now the only way to get to the other side this lake is through it. Fortunately, you see a small boat along the lakeshore. Before you climb in, you feel really nervous because you don't how to swim. Not knowing how to swim is like having your parents' divorce, or having just been harmed by someone. You don't know what to do, how to act or what to believe in.

You get up the courage to jump into the boat with no lifejacket and start to row to the other side. All of the sudden, out of nowhere, a strong wind starts to rock the boat. You try frantically to do all you can to not have this boat tip over, unfortunately, it does anyway. What do you do? Can you save yourself if you don't how to swim? No. You will need someone who knows how to swim to save you. An Earthly Guardian Angel is that someone that will save you from drowning in your thoughts, in your despair, in your unforgiveness and in your life.

Sometimes, the difference between life and death could be having an Earthly Guardian Angel. Your angel can help you stay on your path and help you make the hard decisions. Your angel can encourage you on the good ideas and discourage you on the bad.

Learn to Swim

When your boat tips over in the middle of the lake and you don't how to swim and your Earthly Guardian Angel helps save you, that's great. However, it is important that you learn how to swim so that you can cross other lakes along your path in the future. The best gift an Earthly Guardian Angel can give you is to teach you how to swim. When he or she teaches you ideas, principles and concepts, it is important you apply these teachings in your life. As you do, you will start building confidence in yourself and start trusting your own feelings and insights.

Why is learning to swim so important? We don't want to rely so heavily on this Earthly Guardian Angel that we believe we can't succeed without our angel. When I found myself drowning, Cindy was there a lot at the beginning. Over time, it became less and less necessary to call her, as I started trusting my own feelings. An Earthly Guardian Angel is there to help you start believing in yourself and make you stronger.

God is always there

A Second Kind of Guardian Angel

If you are finding it hard to think of someone that will help you here on Earth, pray and ask God to send you someone. If you ask, He will send you someone. It may not be tomorrow or next week, but keep asking and He will send you someone perfect here on Earth. If you find your situation dire, God may send you the second type of guardian angel, like a deceased relative—like He did for me in the park.

Our Heavenly Father and Jesus Christ know everything. They know what you need and when you need it. But they can't be physically in two places at once, for they have a body just like ours. Therefore, they delegate to relatives on the other side (which build strong family bonds on both sides of the veil) that have the understanding and strength you need at the time.

Guardian angels on the other side of the veil that can assist us here are typically deceased family members. Through Jesus Christ's direction, they will assist us when we ask and are in need of help. Don't let Satan convince you that you are here all alone on Earth. With our Heavenly Father and Jesus Christ and those that have gone before us, we are never alone.

You're All Alone

Prayer

Though our Heavenly Father knows our needs and wants, He has to wait until we ask Him. If our Heavenly Father were to give us everything we need, when we need it, without Him being asked, then it would be intruding on our free agency. Through prayer, all of our wants, needs, desires and dreams can be granted to us—if they are right and if we ask. In the Bible there are over a dozen Scriptures that speak of "ask and ye shall receive" because it is so important that we ask in order to receive.

There may be times that you didn't ask for something, but it was granted anyway. Most likely, in those times others were praying for you. If others pray for us, it allows our Heavenly Father to answer those prayers, without taking away our free agency. Prayer is so powerful; it can help us bridge any gaps in our life that needs to be bridged.

Prayer is not just important so that we may have our wants and needs fulfilled. It is also a way our Heavenly Father can help us without taking away our free agency. When I was about nineteen, I would often drive between my brother's home and the home I was staying at. This drive involved going through a canyon with sharp turns every hundred feet, no streetlights, no place to pull over and only two very narrow lanes.

Late one night, when I was feeling particularly tired, I said a prayer to get home safely. I was doing okay staying awake until about halfway through the canyon. I fell asleep at the wheel and moments before I drove off this cliff, something woke me up and I was able to turn in time. I believe, because I prayed for safety, our Heavenly Father answered my prayers without taking away my free agency or delivering the natural consequences of me driving off a cliff because I fell asleep.

If we pray, He can prompt us before something bad happens, strengthen us when we are tempted and inspire someone else to assist us with our needs. Prayer has the power to guide us through any extremely difficult obstacle course without taking away our free agency. Prayer enables us to make it back home no matter what happens in our lives.

Our Heavenly Father answers prayers in one of two ways. First, through the Spirit by directing us personally through insights, ideas and feelings. Second, through other people. Our Heavenly Father uses others in our lives to answer our prayers. He does this because He can't come down Himself and answer and it gives others the opportunity to serve. With that said, when you pray for our Heavenly Father to help you with a certain need, trial, or challenge, make sure your eyes are open to all possibilities. Some people don't recognize that He has answered them because they are looking for the prayer to be answered in a certain way. Answers come in many forms, so be open to all possibilities.

Belief in God

I hope I have restored your faith in God through clarifying who is to blame when other humans hurt us. Believing in God, His plan, His Gospel, the quest He has sent you on, and His eternal reward for you is far more important than any other belief you will have need of on Earth. Belief in God brings unshaken hope.

If we believe in God, then we will believe in His plan. If we believe in His plan, then we will believe He has restored His Gospel through Jesus Christ on Earth. If we believe He has restored His Gospel on Earth through Jesus Christ, then we can believe He has given us a way home through the atonement. If we believe in the atonement and the other tools (like the armor of God that He spoke of in the Preexistence), then He must have given us strengths, gifts, talents and other things that will help us achieve our quest. If we believe all these things, then we can believe that our family was also handpicked for us, as well as our trials. All together, we can believe He made us strong enough for anything.

Belief in God helps us to believe in our own abilities to succeed. If we can believe that we can succeed on our quest, then we have greatly diminished Satan's power over us. Once we diminish Satan's power over us, we can conquer him and return home with honor as heirs to the Kingdom of God. Belief in God is so powerful that it will start a ripple effect into everything else that we must believe in order to return home.

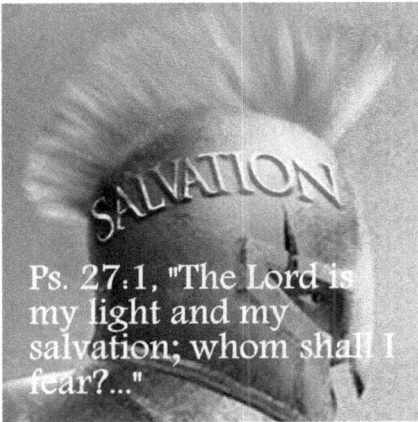

The helmet of salvation (hope) is essential in any battle, especially the one against Satan. If we do not have hope that our efforts will be rewarded, Satan will use that to create fear and doubt in ourselves and in God. Put on the helmet of hope and believe with God's help you can achieve anything, including a throne.

Ps. 27:1, "The Lord is my light and my salvation; whom shall I fear?..."

Believe in God and yourself. Have faith and hope that, through the atonement of Jesus Christ, you can conquer your quest. Reach out to those here on Earth that can assist you when times get hard and pray. Ask God for the things you're in need of. Anyone can make it home if they seek God's counsel, follow His guidance, strive to do better, accept the assistance of others and believe in themselves.

Your Quest for Hope

Your first quest is to determine if you have hope. Hope for things to be good or better, hope that you can overcome your obstacles and hope that you can make it home victorious. If you find that some of your hopes are lacking, write down why and then seek to correct them.

Your second quest is to find someone in your life that can be your Earthly Guardian Angel. Someone who will listen to you, counsel you, guide you and ultimately teach you how to swim. If you don't have someone, ask our Heavenly Father to send you someone perfect for you.

The third quest is if you are in dire need. Ask God to have family members, on the other side of the veil, help you.

Your last quest is to ask yourself: Do you believe you can conquer Satan and His temptations and return home to God? If you don't believe you can, write down why and then pray and ask God to help change your mind. Your quest is to change that belief and have hope again.

Hope for things that are not seen, but are true.

Believe in God and in yourself.

Find an Earthly Guardian Angel
that can help build you up.

Trust that God will send you what you
need when you need it, as you pray.

The Quest for Happiness

DIVORCE

CONFI

FORGIVENESS

PEACE

FAMILY

CHAPTER 9

The Quest for Happiness
Discover where happiness is

our quest for happiness here on Earth and eternity will be based on the choices you make every day. Our Heavenly Father will try and guide us everyday with the tools He's given us to help us on our quest. Similarly, Satan will try to be our puppeteer everyday to encourage us to give in to temptation. You have a choice everyday to follow our Heavenly Father's plan for happiness here and in eternity, or follow Satan's plan, which is for you to fail on your quest, give up your eternal reward and be as miserable as He is.

Everyday, you will be faced with the struggle between good and evil. Do you choose the path filled with darkness or do you choose the path filled with light? Satan will tempt you to choose the doors full of darkness using the media and poor examples. We must use the tools (the Spirit, armor...) God has given us to discern when Satan is doing this. Satan is not going to show you the obvious darkness on the outside of any door (sin). He is going to show you people looking "free" and having fun.

Watch out for Satan's fiery Darts of Lies!

Sin is Freedom

Just like the caramel apple, Satan will make sin look as tempting and sweet as possible to lure you in. Once Satan has you in, He will close the door behind you, making you think it is locked or that you can't change your mind and leave. Whether you mess up today or tomorrow, you always have a choice to walk back out of that door you were tempted to walk through in the first place. Beware of Satan's plan of deception. He has a funny way of sneaking up on us when we are thinking about making good choices.

When making choices, try to remember why you are here, who you are and where the quest can take you.

Always remember these CORE beliefs:

- Who are you?- A child of God
- Why are you here? – To take a test – go on a quest
- Where will you go when you die? – That's all up to you…

The Power of Now

You have a choice about how your life turns out right now. Things may have happened to you that hurt you deeply. You can't change the past, but you get to decide, in the present, what will impact your future. Blaming your parents, God or anyone else for what you decided to do with your life thus far will not only keep you stuck in the past and lost in the present, but confused about the future. No matter what has happened to you, you have the power and strength within to make different choices, be happy and still conquer the dragon.

Always remember you can't change the past. You might have decided to partake of caramel apples, or others might have hurt you when they abused their free agency. No matter what has happened, you can decide to conquer your quest or give up. If you give up, Satan has won. If you choose right now that you want to get back on your path and move forward as an heir in the Kingdom of God, then you won.

For example: Let's say right now on your quest you have fallen off three cliffs (drugs), two mountainsides (porn), and almost drowned in a lake (suicidal thoughts). You have also been wounded (molested), beaten (physically), and pushed around (bullied). What do you do? Do you let those past moments define who you are, or do you take your life back from Satan and let this next moment define who you are? If you were watching a movie and you saw someone fall off three cliffs, two mountainsides and almost drown in the lake while beaten, wounded and bullied and then he dusted himself off, put on the necessary Band-Aids, and tried again, wouldn't you see him as a hero when he decided his life was worth fighting for, no matter what has happened to him in the past?

> Everyone, until death, is given the opportunity to change, repent and become whole again. If they can achieve the quest, then they will be able to receive everything from our Heavenly Father.

Perspective

Did you know that God saved the best and strongest for last? God needed his strongest spirits to be on Earth before Jesus Christ came again. He knew Satan would use all His power, temptation and evil designs to thwart Christ's plans for return.

Jesus Christ needs us to be as strong as we were in the Preexistence (warriors of light), so as to battle against the evils of Satan and His followers. To prove my point, have you noticed there is more confusion, temptation, evil, abuse and violence now in the world than ever before? Our Heavenly Father knew that each of us was strong enough to overcome Satan and His followers, or else He would not have sent us here when the world would be at its darkest.

Though we have many more obstacles than any others that came before us, God would not have sent us here if we were not strong enough to overcome our obstacles. In fact, God did not just send the strongest, but the most talented, gifted, wisest spirits that He could in order to prepare for Christ's second coming. You have a calling or special quest for this day and age. It may be to help your family or something else. Either way, our Heavenly Father needs you to make good choices with an eternal perspective.

Eternal perspective

What if you could go back to the Preexistence and see yourself conquering this quest. What would that do for you? Would that help you believe that this Earthly life is a test to defeat the dragon of all lies, a test to not partake of any caramel apples, a test to believe in God, despite what others do to us and a test to see if we will push through by using the atonement, no matter what life throws at us.

Why not look at ourselves and our lives with an eternal perspective? If you could plant in your heart that this quest you're on is to prove yourself worthy as a prince or princess to a Heavenly King, wouldn't you fight harder, be better, think wiser and know you could succeed? It's all about perspective. If we could have an eternal perspective on what happens to us in this life then each of us would not sweat the small stuff, but overcome the big stuff and do whatever it takes to fight for the reward.

Let's say you came from a divorced family, with an alcoholic parent and a perverted uncle who had touched you. What would that do to you if you had no idea why you were on Earth? A lot of people would let it define them and they would get into drugs, alcohol, pre-marital sex and even commit suicide. But if you were to have an eternal perspective and look at what happened to you as the results of others' poor choices, and realize that this is one of your trials, wouldn't you try and overcome to be a princess? Wouldn't you press forward, dust yourself off, put Band-Aids on where you need them and then be ready to climb the next mountain? If all of us could look at every trial and challenge as a bump in the road and something we need to learn from, forgive and overcome, wouldn't we use those trials as character builders and stepping stones on our path to receive our eternal reward?

This quest was never meant to be easy—only worth it.

If you knew right now that you agreed in the Preexistence to have the trials in your life, wouldn't that give you the strength and power to overcome them? We would not have agreed to any trial that we could not overcome. Nor, would our Heavenly Father have allowed these challenges to be placed on our path if He didn't think we could overcome them. Satan is the one that wants to blind our eyes, deafen our ears, close our hearts and deaden our minds to the fact that we are on a quest to become princes and princesses in the Kingdom of God. Do not doubt your individual worth and divine destiny, for doubt brings darkness to our minds, which can lead us down dangerous roads.

Doubt

Doubt brings fear. Where there is fear, there is no faith. If we do not have faith that God gave us what we would need to overcome our trials and challenges, then we will not overcome our trials and challenges, but just mask them with all the caramel apples to deaden the pain. Doubt—in ourselves and in God—is one of Satan's greatest tools. Our Heavenly Father has given us the light of Christ to distinguish between right and wrong. Satan knows this and He will have us doubt right after we get an answer from God.

Watch out for Satan's Fiery Darts of Lies!

You can't do it

If we constantly doubt ourselves and the God that sent us, we will find ourselves surrounded by darkness, disbelief, worry and self-esteem problems. Once we stop believing in ourselves, then we start following the crowd. Usually, it's a crowd making poor choices. When you start making poor choices, then Satan feeds you with more doubt that you could ever overcome. When you feel you can't ever change and get back on your path, then you will feel hopeless. Hopelessness occurs where Satan convinces us that there's no purpose to this life, there is no God. So live it up, for when we die that is it.

Satan will try to take us to the darkest areas of our minds, bodies, families and friends, so that he can thwart our potential. Do not let doubt rule your world. Believe in God and yourself and the quest that you're on.

You are Strong Enough

You are strong enough and have the potential of becoming a prince and princess in the Kingdom of God. You have everything you need here on Earth to overcome anything on your quest back home. God has given you strength, talents, gifts, family, forgiveness, atonement, the light of Christ, the armor of God, the Gospel of Christ, guardian angels, prayer and everything else you would ever need to conquer the dragon and come out victorious.

It is never too late to change. Though darkness may surround you, you always have a choice. God made sure you have a way through to bring brighter skies, better food, happier victories and an eternal perspective. We are strong enough to defeat Satan and win our reward.

My Quest for Happiness

I am the eleventh of twelve children, and yet, I never felt part of a family. I have lived with six different families, moved thirty times up to my thirtieth year and have been confused about a lot of things in my life. After I ran away from my mom, I went to live with my dad for two years. During my senior year he and my step-mom got a divorce, so I moved. I moved in with a friend for six months. Because there wasn't permanent room for me, I moved in with another family.

I felt very lost and alone. I didn't know where I belonged, who to talk to, or what my future looked like. I was hurt often by those I considered close friends through gossip, lies and guys. I was glad when high school was over so I could start fresh in a new area and in a new part of my life.

The first year out of high school, I lived with my brother, but I still wasn't very happy. I decided to move back with my mom and try that out. That lasted about a month. We still did not see eye to eye. While I was feeling lost and alone, one of my sisters mentioned to me a course she had taken. A course that had helped her forgive those who had harmed her, reconnect with God and discover who she really was.

I went to this three-day course and felt enlightened and uplifted. It had nothing to do with what they did, but with what they taught. They taught me what I'm teaching you, except mine includes the purpose of life. We must forgive those who have harmed us. If we don't, darkness will always follow. We must believe in ourselves and in the God that sent us. We must love our family no matter what. We must make sure there are safe boundaries for us in all our relationships. Good choices will always bring us joy and poor choices always make our life harder.

I always had a relationship with God and believed He had a purpose for me here on Earth. But, I became the happiest when I realized I didn't have to be perfect, that forgiving others is a must and that I was strong enough for any trial or challenge that comes my way. Once you accept and believe that you are here on a quest, then you can be happy no matter what happens in your life through forgiving those who have harmed you and getting close to God.

Your Quest for Happiness

Your **first quest** is to discover why you're unhappy. Are you unhappy because old thoughts still consume your mind with pain and hurt? Are you unhappy because you still don't feel you can conquer your quest? Are you unhappy because you feel there's no way to come back? Once you have discovered why you're unhappy you have the power in this moment to change your perspective, tell Satan to go to hell and start making better choices.

Post on your wall what good choices you will now be making.

Your **second quest** is to start making better choices. That begins with looking at life with an eternal perspective. For example: If your parents are divorced, look at that as something you can learn to do differently. If you have been harmed by another, see what you can learn from it, forgive them and help others not have the same thing happen to them. Start taking a look at how you can use your trials and challenges as building blocks and stepping-stones to reach greater heights.

Changing your perspective to an eternal one will alter how you overcome things now.

Your **third quest** is to look for areas in your life where you have doubt. If you are doubting, then why? Do not feel strong enough? Do you feel you can't change? Do you feel God won't help you? Discover how you can change it from doubt to faith. You can also ask God to help increase your faith and believe in yourself more.

Your fourth quest is to be happy. When you doubt, fear, make poor choices and use an Earthly perspective you will not find happiness no matter your circumstances. If you can look at everything as a challenge that you accepted, you be able to have confidence in yourself now—for you knew at one time (Preexistence) that you could overcome anything. Find good things that make you happy and try to do them everyday.

Today's the day. Now is the time
to change your perspective.

Have faith in God and in yourself
that you can overcome anything.

Remember to cheer yourself on during
trials, for you can be the prince or
princess God wants you to be.

The Quest for Eternal Life

CHAPTER 10

The Quest for Eternal Life
Discover your truest potential

*H*opefully, by now, you've realized that this Earthly life is a test. Will we follow our Heavenly Father by making good choices and using the atonement, or we will, instead, follow Satan, give in to temptation and make poor choices?

Every choice—big and small—counts on this Earth. If we make small good choices, then the big choices will be easier to make wisely. On the other hand, if we make poor small choices, then the big choices will reach the same outcome.

> Our quest here on Earth will be full of choices every day. And those choices will lead us down certain paths. The question is which path will you choose?

> The path that will lead you back to your Heavenly King and obtain your eternal reward because you defeated the dragon?

> The path that is easy, well-trodden, filled with caramel apples, riotous living, selfish desires and poor choices?

> Or the path that has some rough terrain, but nothing too difficult because you don't want to put forth too much energy?

Every Earthly quest will be rewarded. Of course, some rewards will be better than others. Our Heavenly Father made sure that everyone would be judged fairly according to his/her works and deeds on Earth. Therefore there are three degrees of glory, or three different kingdoms, that will be homes to everyone on Earth, depending on the individual's bravery during the quest.

The Afterlife

We have already discussed where we lived before we came to Earth. In the Preexistence, all those who fought on the Savior's side became knighted with a body and blessed with free agency. Once we came to Earth, we were placed on a path with unique trials and challenges, but also with unique strengths, talents and gifts. Our choices here will determine where we live after we die—for eternity. In other words, we passed our first test in the Preexistence, so we are given the opportunity to take the second test here on Earth. Our performance on the second test will determine where we are placed for eternity.

Once we die, we will be judged on how we did on this Earth, as stated in Rev 2:23, "...I am He which searcheth the reins and hearts: and I will give unto every one of you according to your works." Therefore, how much you prove yourself worthy here on Earth will determine which kingdom you will obtain.

Death is not the end, but merely a type of beginning.

Spirit World

Once you die, your spirit and body will be separated. Your body is laid in the grave where it remains temporarily. Your spirit moves on to the Spirit World. If you've ever been to a funeral viewing you may have noticed that the deceased person does not look natural. The body looks like something is missing. Our bodies house our spirits. Once we die, our body becomes empty.

Our spirit goes to place called the Spirit World. The Spirit World is divided into two parts: Spirit Paradise and Spirit Prison. There are some religions that believe the spirit world is divided into Heaven and Hell and that it is the final resting place of our spirits. That is not the case. The spirit world is a waiting place for the final judgment, a place where there is still constant learning and growth.

You may ask why we would need a waiting place before we are judged. God is a fair and just God. There are many people on Earth that never got a chance to hear the Gospel of Jesus Christ, be baptized and try to live as He lived. So for God to be a fair and just God, He will need to give them the chance in the spirit world to accept or reject the Gospel. The spirit world makes it possible for every human to have a chance to accept or reject Jesus Christ and His Gospel. It says this perfectly in 1 Pet. 4:6 where it states, "For this cause was the gospel preached also to them that are dead, that they might be judged according to men in the flesh, but live according to God in the spirit."

Spirit Prison

Because God is a fair God He will not place good and bad people in the same dimension while waiting for final judgment. Those who will go to spirit prison made bad choices, hurt others, committed sins or ate of the caramel apples and did not repent while on Earth. They took the road most traveled with riotous living, selfish desires, feeding constantly on caramel apples and having no thought or desire to believe in Jesus Christ.

Spirit Prison could be referred to as a hell for there will not be much joy. Those in Spirit Prison will realize that they had wasted their life doing whatever they felt like doing to themselves, their bodies and to others. Those who dwell here are those who did not think they would have to answer for their choices of hurting themselves and others while on Earth.

This part of the Spirit World will not have much light. Those who dwell here will emanate darkness. It will be filled with people who have regrets, shame, anger and guilt. It will be filled with all those who did not take their quest seriously and were defeated by the dragon.

Though many have lost their way on Earth and did not receive the opportunity to hear Christ's Gospel, the Gospel will be preached in Spirit Prison to give everyone an equal chance to be redeemed through Christ. In 1 Pet. 3:19 it states, "By which also he went and preached unto the spirits in prison;"

Spirit Paradise

All those in Spirit Paradise made good choices, tried the best they could while on their quest, helped those in need, have repented, picked themselves up when they fell and tried to follow the example of Jesus Christ. Jesus Christ spoke of Spirit Paradise in Luke 23:43, "And Jesus said unto him, Verily I say unto thee, today shalt thou be with me in paradise."

This part of the spirit world will be filled with light. Those who dwell here will be full of love, joy, forgiveness, and compassion. It will be all those who took their quest seriously, endured to the end, put on and took off Band-Aids as needed, reached out to help others on their quest and truly wanted to be a prince or princess in God's Kingdom.

Judgment Day

On Judgment Day, you will be brought before God to be judged according to your works and deeds while on your quest. As stated in Romans 14:10, "...For we shall all stand before the judgment seat of Christ." God will search through your life and see what mountains you climbed, where you've repented, how much you've helped others, if you've served your family and where justice and mercy will have claim on you.

Each of us will stand in front of God and be judged according to our works, as stated in Matt 16:27, "For the Son of man shall come in the glory of his Father with his angels; and then he shall reward every man according to his works." We will each stand beside Jesus Christ, who will be our attorney or advocate as mentioned in 1 Jn. 2:1, "...And if any man sin, we have an advocate with the Father, Jesus Christ the righteous."

Jesus Christ will plead your case, telling how much you've repented and tried to do what was right during your mortal life, or Earthly quest. For instance, let's say every mountain you climbed you fell off (partook of sin), but you dusted yourself off, repented and tried again. When those sins come up during your life's review, Jesus Christ will speak up and say you have repented of those sins and, through the atonement, you have been forgiven. That sin will then be wiped clean.

In John 3:17 it states, "For God sent not his Son into the world to condemn the world; but that the world through him might be saved." Jesus Christ our Savior came to save the world and will use the atonement to wipe away every sin we have committed as long as we repent. Our Heavenly Father and Jesus Christ knew we would not be perfect. They knew we would fall down, get hurt and deeply wounded on our quest. They made a way through the atonement for us to pick ourselves up, bridge the gap of imperfection, heal any wound and start again.

Every time a sin comes up during the review of your life on judgment day, Jesus Christ will plead your case if you repented. He will say, "I have paid for his/her sins when I was on the Earth. He/she has repented of those things he/she did wrong and I have made up the difference between his/her imperfections in my perfection. I have made him/her perfect through me."

Jesus Christ paved the way for all of us to be saved and earn an eternal reward as prince or princesses in the Kingdom of God, as stated in Acts 4:12, "Neither is there salvation in any other: for there is none other name under heaven given among men, whereby we must be saved." All our Heavenly Father and Jesus Christ ask is that we do our best, repent when we have fallen, help those in need, try and follow Christ's example and get back on track.

Eternal Worlds or Kingdoms

After you've been judged according to your works and how much you've repented, you will be resurrected. Your spirit and body will be reunited and made perfect. Not one hair from your head will be lost, any physical deformities will be restored and you will return to a more youthful body. You will find that, once you are reunited with your body, you will feel complete and full of joy.

In Phil. 3:21 we read, "Who shall change our vile body, that it may be fashioned like unto his glorious body, according to the working whereby he is able even to subdue all things unto himself." Our resurrected body will receive the glory according to how well we did on our quest while on Earth. Your resurrected body will receive the same brightness as the kingdom you earned.

Dependent upon your choices, you will be placed in one of three kingdoms: the Telestial, Terrestrial or Celestial kingdom, or in outer darkness. These kingdoms are referenced in John 14:2-3 were it states,

"In my Father's house are many mansions: if it were not so, I would have told you. I go to prepare a place for you." And in 1 Cor. 15:40-41, "There are also celestial bodies, and bodies terrestrial: but the glory of the celestial is one, and the glory of the terrestrial is another. 41. There is one glory of the sun, and another glory of the moon, and another glory of the stars: for one star differeth from another star in glory." As stated, each kingdom has a different degree of brightness and glory.

Telestial Kingdom

The lowest kingdom is called the telestial kingdom. It is compared to the brightness of the stars, as stated in 1 Cor. 15:41, "...another glory of the stars: for one star differeth from another star in glory." Those who will be placed here are those that wanted nothing to do with their own quest and were determined to try to make others fail on theirs. They ate every caramel apple placed in front of them and let the dragon, Satan, be their puppeteer.

Those who will be placed in the telestial kingdom are those who murdered, lied, raped, stole, committed adultery...It is a place for those evil people who followed Satan and His designs by hurting others and wanted nothing to do with the Savior or Heavenly Father's plan.

Those who dwell here are those who looked for every opportunity while on their quest, to hurt others, eat only caramel apples, abuse their bodies and any other act that either put them on top through selfish designs or indulged in every indulgence while on Earth. This kingdom will be similar to Earth. It will have its beauty but far, far less than the beauty of the other higher kingdoms.

This kingdom will hold less power, joy, love and unity than the other higher kingdoms. Those who dwell here will receive unto themselves what they have done unto others (i.e., darkness begets darkness, hate begets hate.) Those who dwell here did not repent and rejected the Gospel of Jesus Christ and as a result will suffer as Christ suffered for the wrongs they did unto others and themselves. This kingdom will have the visitation of the Holy Ghost and no other.

Terrestrial Kingdom

The middle kingdom is called the terrestrial kingdom. It will be as bright as the moon, as referenced in 1 Cor. 15:40-41, "and the glory of the terrestrial is another...glory of the moon..." Those who are rewarded or placed in this kingdom are those who took their quest lightly. They would tread lightly on slightly bumpy roads and would put on Band-Aids when needed but not take them off (not forgive everyone). They repented when they found it convenient. It is a place for honorable people who didn't try to harm others, sometimes only themselves.

They repented of some things but didn't repent of others. They knew and loved Jesus Christ but they kept their favorite sins or ate their favorite caramel apples. They didn't want to completely give up what was necessary to follow Christ and climb every mountain placed before them because they wanted things to be easy.

This kingdom will be like the Garden of Eden where the colors and plant life will be beautiful, but far less than the highest kingdom. This kingdom will have more power, love and joy than the telestial kingdom, but far less than the celestial kingdom. Those who are awarded this kingdom will be happy and content, but will not receive a fullness of joy and peace with their families like unto those in the celestial kingdom. This kingdom will receive visits from the Savior Jesus Christ.

Celestial Kingdom

The highest kingdom is called the celestial kingdom as referenced in 1 Cor. 15:40-41, "There are also celestial bodies...the glory of the celestial is one...There is one glory of the sun..." This kingdom is compared to the glory of the sun and where we will receive all that the Father has as stated in Rev. 21:7, "He that overcometh shall inherit all things..." This is where our Heavenly Father lives. This is the kingdom where we will receive our eternal reward as princes and princesses in the

Kingdom of God. It is our ultimate goal. Here, we will be rewarded everything because we defeated the dragon and endured to the end.

Those who are rewarded the celestial kingdom will find true peace and ultimate joy with their families and loved ones who also made it there. In Ps 16:11 it speaks of true joy, "Thou wilt show me the path of life: in thy presence is fullness of joy; at thy right hand there are pleasures for evermore." Not only will you have a fullness of joy in this kingdom, but it will be far more beautiful, vibrant and alive than any other kingdom or human could imagine.

The celestial kingdom holds all power, love, peace and creation that no other kingdom will possess. This kingdom is for those who defeated the dragon, helped others in need, went the extra mile, put on and took off every Band-Aid when wounded (forgiven all) and completely loved Jesus Christ. Because they loved Jesus Christ they truly believed in His Gospel, received all of His ordinances, completely followed Him, tried to do His will above their own and did all that they had to do in order to come out victorious in the end.

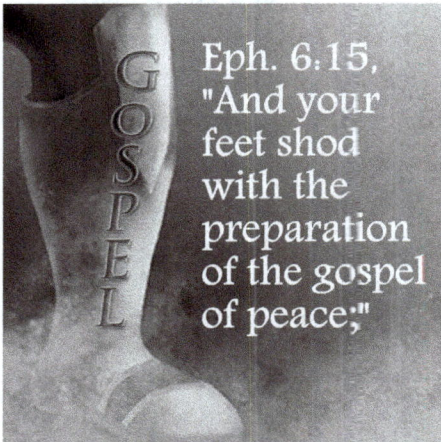

Eph. 6:15, "And your feet shod with the preparation of the gospel of peace;"

GOSPEL

These are those who wore the shoes of the Gospel (i.e., faith, repentance, baptism, all ordinances) on their quest in order to get through it successfully. For they knew without shoes they would not be able to climb certain mountains or tread over certain terrain. They used the shoes of the Gospel to overcome all obstacles and defeat the dragon.

Those who receive eternal life with our Heavenly Father climbed every mountain that was placed before them and returned with honor. And as a result they will be crowned as heirs in the Kingdom of God, as stated in 2 Tim. 4:8, "Henceforth there is laid up for me a crown of righteousness, which the Lord, the righteous judge, shall give me at that day: and not to me only, but unto all them also that love his appearing." These are they who will be told in the end, "Well done thou good and faithful son or daughter, receive your reward."

Outer Darkness

In addition to the three kingdoms, there is also a place called outer darkness, as referenced in Matt 8:12, "But the children of the kingdom shall be cast out into outer darkness: there shall be weeping and gnashing of teeth." This is where Satan and His followers will dwell. Those humans that will be cast down into outer darkness are those who received a witness of Jesus Christ, had His Gospel, knew it was true by the witness of the Holy Ghost, and then denied it (Satan and his followers in the Preexistence and those like Judas Iscariot, who was one of Jesus' apostles, who betrayed Him).

For example, those who dwell here will have received a witness that the quest is real, that Jesus Christ is the Savior and Redeemer of the world, had on the full armor of God, received all the ordinances of the Gospel, and then denied it, joined teams with Satan and fully rebelled against God. Not many Earthly beings will go to this realm because they would've had to have a personal witness from the Holy Ghost of Jesus Christ being the Savior of the World and then rebelled against Christ and lead others down dark paths.

Humans that are cast down into outer darkness are basically those who have sold their soul to Satan and help Satan try to destroy others on their quest by deceiving them and leading them away from Jesus Christ and His Gospel. This realm is full of darkness for it holds no joy, love, compassion, or any other good attribute and is known as Hell. Hell is a place full of unquenchable fire, wailing and gnashing of teeth and complete and utter hopelessness.

The Choice is Yours

Though your quest may be hard because of rough terrain (free agency), steep mountains (family dysfunction), raging waters (violence), deep wounds (unforgiveness) and sometimes impossible obstacle courses (addiction), God has not left us alone. He gave us everything we would need here on Earth in order to conquer our quest and become heirs in His Kingdom. If you find yourself not succeeding, ask yourself why? Have you used every tool God has giving you? Do you believe in God? Do you believe in yourself? If you can answer yes to those three questions then you are strong enough to complete this quest victoriously.

You only have one shot at this quest while on Earth. Those who did not hear about the Gospel of Jesus Christ or about the armor of God will be given that opportunity in the spirit world, but will still be judged on how they treated their bodies, themselves and others. Remember, everyone was given the light of Christ to differentiate between right and wrong.

You are a child of God and are of royal birth. You have been placed on Earth, knighted with a body, to be tested and tried in order to see if you are worthy of being an heir in His Kingdom.

> What you do here on Earth will determine
> where you will live for eternity.

Are you ready for your Earthly quest as a prince or princess of the Heavenly King to defeat the dragon in your life that will try to burn your future? The choice is yours to open your eyes and see why you are here and what you're capable of. God has given us the armor of God, including, the Sword of the Spirit, to defeat the dragon of lies to win the battle of life. Ask yourself: Will you come out conqueror and victorious in the end?

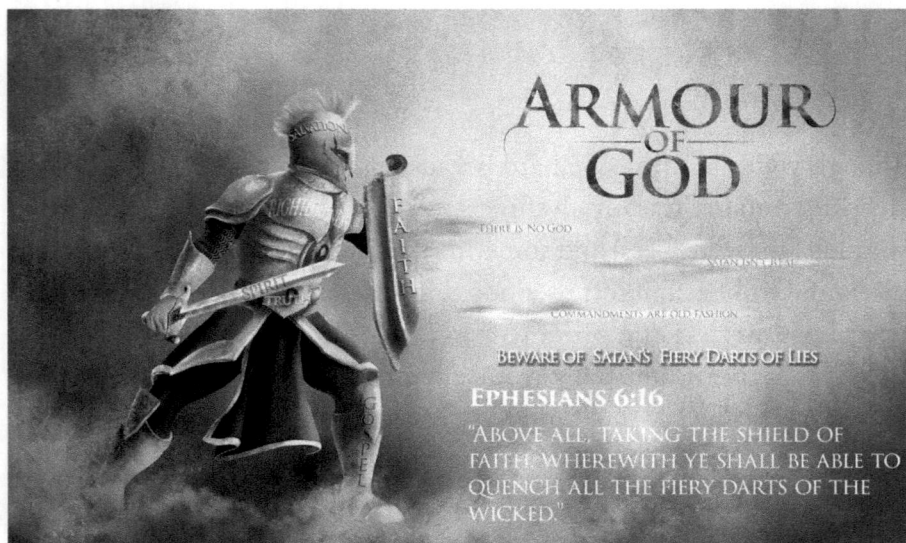

ARMOUR
—OF—
GOD

THERE IS NO GOD

A MAN ON CROSS

COMMANDMENTS ARE OLD FASHION

BEWARE OF SATAN'S FIERY DARTS OF LIES

EPHESIANS 6:16
"ABOVE ALL, TAKING THE SHIELD OF
FAITH, WHEREWITH YE SHALL BE ABLE TO
QUENCH ALL THE FIERY DARTS OF THE
WICKED."

Your Final Quest

Your final and most important quest: Is to ask: Is the information I have shared true? Your job is to find out through prayer if what I have talked about is true. Ask our Heavenly Father, if you are on this Earth to be tested, and if the spirit world and kingdoms are real. When you get the answer that this quest is real, that life has a purpose and we are strong enough, I hope you become more determined to discover the Gospel of Jesus Christ, live within its teachings, put on the full armor of God and become, once again, a warrior of light and truth so that you may be strong enough to defeat the dragon of all lies and return home as a true and tried prince or princess in the Kingdom of God.

This Quest is but a small moment in time.

You succeeded once. You can succeed again.

The Ultimate Quest

Terrestrial Kingdom

Outer Darkness

Celestial Kingdom

Telestial Kingdom

- The Real Test Begins -

Your quest truly begins when you start applying the principles taught in this book. To ultimately conquer Satan, the Dragon, we must start with the belief that we are of Royal birth. Once we believe we have the potential of being a Prince or Princess in the Kingdom of God, than that belief can fuel all of our other beliefs, efforts, actions and ultimately bring transformation. Transformation from an ordinary human to a warrior sent on a quest to defeat the dragon, overcome obstacles and prove ourselves worthy as heirs in the Kingdom of God.

There is a power within each of us to change or to continue to win the fight. There is also a power that comes from sharing your experiences with each other to motivate, inspire, uplift and bring hope to those that don't think they can defeat the dragon. Therefore, I would like to extend an invitation to all those would like to share how they have conquered the dragon in their own life, overcome obstacles, learned from trials and challenges and or perhaps, seen a whole new world open up to them from embracing these truths spoken of in *You're Strong Enough*.

If you would like to share please visit

http://www.kassipontious.com/quest-results.html

I welcome and will post the experiences shared, so that we may build each other up and help others realize that our enemy is the dragon, not each other.

I would like to start by sharing a song from *JASON MRAZ*. This song is posted on my website: www.kassipontious.com under music and the lyrics are below, with additions of my own for emphasis in italicized and in parenthesis. If you can picture our Heavenly Father or Jesus Christ singing this to you, it can be a very powerful tool when you feel discouraged.

When I look into your eyes *(divine nature)*
It's like watching the night sky
Or a beautiful sunrise *(your special)*
Well, there's so much they hold *(power)*
And just like them old stars *(past relatives)*
I see that you've come so far *(growth)*
To be right where you are *(your path)*
How old is your soul? *(Preexistence)*

Well, I won't give up on us *(you and the Savior)*
Even if the skies get rough *(trials and challenges)*
I'm giving you all my love *(atonement)*
I'm still looking up *(up toward your potential)*

And when you're needing your space *(to make your own choices)*
To do some navigating *(deciding who you are)*
I'll be here patiently waiting
To see what you find *(your choice – free agency)*

'Cause even the stars they burn
Some even fall to the earth *(making mistakes)*
We've got a lot to learn *(earth test)*
God knows we're worth it *(divine nature)*

No, I won't give up (*it's never too late to change*)
I don't wanna be someone who walks away so easily
I'm (*The Savior*) here to stay and make the difference that I can make (*atonement*)
Our differences they do a lot to teach us how to use
The tools and gifts (*from God*) we got, yeah, we got a lot at stake (*this life is a test*)
And in the end, you're still my friend (*you and the Savior*) at least we did intend
For us to work we didn't break, we didn't burn *(we are strong enough)*
We had to learn how to bend (*change*) without the world caving in (*giving up on yourself*)
I had to learn what I got (*strengths*), and what I'm not (*worthless*), and who I am (*child of a king*)

I won't give up on us
Even if the skies get rough (*you make mistakes*)
I'm giving you all my love (*the Atonement*)
I'm still looking up, still looking up (*up toward your potential*)

Well, I won't give up (No I'm not) on us (Giving up)
God knows I'm tough (I am tough), he knows (I am loved)
We got a lot (We're alive) to learn (We are loved)
God knows we're worth it (And we're worth it)

I won't give up on us *(you and the Savior)*
Even if the skies get rough *(you make mistakes)*
I'm giving you all my love *(atonement)*
I'm still looking up *(up toward your potential)*

JASON MRAZ - I WON'T GIVE UP LYRICS

Everyone can make it back home to our Heavenly Father as heirs in His Kingdom if we put forth our best effort and use all the tools God has given us. If you would like more information on my beliefs please visit www.kassipontious.com

We each are strong enough for
our life here on Earth.

You succeeded once. You can succeed again.

If you enjoyed this book, please consider posting a review on Amazon. I read all reviews and very much appreciate your thoughts and comments.

Connect with Kassi L. Pontious
Website: http://www.kassipontious.com/
Facebook: https://www.facebook.com/AuthorKassiLPontious
Twitter: https://twitter.com/KassiPontious
Also by Kassi L. Pontious
You're Powerful Enough - coming soon
You're Brave Enough – coming soon

www.ingramcontent.com/pod-product-compliance
Lightning Source LLC
Chambersburg PA
CBHW061719020426
42331CB00006B/1000